TRACKING HUMANS

TRACKING HUMANS

A Fundamental Approach to Finding Missing Persons,
Insurgents, Guerillas, and Fugitives from the Law

David Diaz
with V.L. McCann

Lyons Press
Guilford, Connecticut
An imprint of Globe Pequot Press

Excerpt on page 13 from "The Elephant's Child," by Rudyard Kipling.

Excerpt on page 21 from *The Anatomy of Human Destructiveness,* by Erich Fromm.

Excerpt on page 81 from "Burnt Norton" from *Four Quartets* by T.S. Eliot.

Excerpt on page 111 from *Selected Essays* by Samuel Johnson.

Text Design: Sheryl P. Kober
Layout: Mary Ballachino

ISBN 978-0-7627-8442-4

Printed in the United States of America
10 9 8 7 6 5 4 3 2 1

The Library of Congress has previously catalogued an earlier (hardcover) edition as follows:

Diaz, David, 1959-
    Tracking—signs of man, signs of hope : a systematic approach to the art and science of tracking humans / David Diaz with V. L. McCann.
        p. cm.
    Includes bibliographical references and index.
    ISBN 1-59228-686-0 (trade paper)
    1. Missing persons—Investigation. 2. Forensic sciences. 3. Criminal investigation. I. McCann, V. L.   II. Title.
    HV6762.A3D52 2005
    363.2'336—dc22

                                                                    2005006063

Dedicated to the missing and exploited children throughout the world and to those members of the American Armed Forces who were, are, or ever will be held as prisoners of war or declared missing in action.

The instinct of man is to pursue everything that flies from him, and to fly from all that pursue him.

—Voltaire

CONTENTS

FOREWORD

In this period, when modern armies are uncompromisingly reshaping their respective forces to face the challenges and threats of the twenty-first century in a high-tech mindset, the primordial principles of tracking still prove their responsiveness, in the same way as when human beings still hunted for their food. *Tracking Humans* rekindles the light and illuminates the path toward the need to relearn the skills of tracking. Above and beyond, this book will certainly trigger the conceptualization of new sensors and surveillance equipment for improved combat effectiveness.

During my stint as commander, 18th Infantry Battalion, Philippine Army, I had the chance to train with SFC David Diaz on Basilan Island, Philippines, during bilateral military exercises in 2002. David was called upon to share his expertise on tracking with the members of the battalion because we both believe that, indeed, *tracking matters*. His same training program was reintroduced into the Philippine Army and has been successfully and aggressively implemented ever since.

Lt. Col. Daniel Lucero
18th Infantry Battalion
Philippine Army

Dave Diaz is an acknowledged expert on tracking and field craft, recognized throughout the US Army's Special Operations community. His methods have proven themselves through success by empowering soldiers to effectively track armed combatants during the Global War on Terror. Dave's book is an excellent digest of his validated methods of instruction and techniques. I'd recommend it as a "must read" for all field soldiers and trainers. It provides invaluable tools to execute stand-alone tracking courses or enhance sniper or reconnaissance programs.

CSM John G. Macejunas
US Army (Retired)

Tracking Humans by David Diaz is probably the most succinct tactical/ tracking writing that I have ever had the pleasure of reading. It offers something for everyone, from outdoorsman, policeman, and rescue personnel to SPECOPS operator. It allows the reader to gain valuable insight into techniques and methods that when practiced will significantly increase survivability and effectiveness, depending on the use. As a twenty-six-year Army veteran, seventeen-plus of which was as a SOF operator, I highly recommend this book for those serious about operating in the field, whether you are a soldier, law enforcement officer, or rescue professional.

CW3 MICHAEL HAUGEN
1ST SPECIAL FORCES GROUP (AIRBORNE)
FORT LEWIS, WASHINGTON, US ARMY

Tactical tracking has become a critical skill for the Global War on Terror, and only a handful of people have the expertise and experience of Dave Diaz. I had the good fortune of working with Dave on Basilan Island, Philippines, in the spring and summer of 2001. Dave had worked on me for months with his ideas of how tracking could be applied to our efforts there. He changed the way we looked at everything and made our detachment realize the importance of understanding "everything." What Dave really taught us was Intelligence Preparation of the Battlefield (IPB) to the square inch. Dave teaches his Trackers to collect data in all types of terrain, weather, and culture in the area of operation. This data is then analyzed to the point where it becomes instinctual to the Tracker.

Dave became a surrogate member of our team in the Philippines and planned, coordinated, and executed a six-week tracker course for the Filipino soldiers we were advising. The results of his course were nothing short of astounding. In six weeks, he took these soldiers from barely being able to pass an army physical fitness test to completing an extremely demanding field training exercise. The soldiers were taught techniques for collecting tracking data and how to apply that data to actual tracking. Some of the soldiers became so proficient in their tracking that they could track on their hands and knees during hours of limited visibility.

The most visible change was the soldier's situational awareness (culture, terrain, and weather) and attention to detail in every task (especially tracking reports that would help commanders make informed decisions). The skills and techniques Dave teaches can be applied from the jungles of the Philippines to the deserts of the Middle East and will keep soldiers alive as well as bring terrorists to justice.

CAPTAIN MICHAEL PERRY
1ST SPECIAL FORCES GROUP (AIRBORNE)
FORT LEWIS, WASHINGTON, US ARMY

INTRODUCTION

Tracker. The very word forms images of buckskin-clad braves crouching over the ground, carefully studying the signs before them. It brings back memories of old cavalry movies where the dust-worn officers watch and wait while the scout reaches out his hand, touches the hoofprint near his foot, stands up, and points to the horizon declaring, "South. Three days' ride." It is an image that fills the average person with awe and wonder. How does the scout know which way they're heading? How does he know the print is three days old?

In the movie *Butch Cassidy and the Sundance Kid,* Butch and Sundance try every trick they know to shake the slow, steady advance of their pursuers. They double up on one horse, watching with surprise when the posse divides in two and then quickly comes back together again—dead on their trail. "Who are these guys?" they keep asking. After setting off on foot, they watch in disbelief as a famed Indian scout tracks them over solid rock. "How does he do that?" they ask again.[1]

But is there really a shroud of mystery behind the skills of a native-born Tracker? Are only a select few endowed with the sacred ability to track animals or human beings through miles of rock, brush, or jungle? I am here to tell you that there is no mystery to tracking, and I will prove to you that these skills can be learned by almost anyone.

But why write a book on tracking? Our technologically advanced society has eliminated the need for such rudimentary search methods, right? Little known to many in America, people all over the world still use these techniques, and specialized training in the field of tracking is essential for many agencies in our own country to accomplish their missions. The military uses some of these skills in areas of direct combat, guerrilla warfare, strategic reconnaissance, VIP rescue, and downed pilot recovery. The success of a search and rescue team most assuredly depends

---

1 George Roy Hill, dir., *Butch Cassidy and the Sundance Kid,* Twentieth Century Fox, 1969.

on the team's ability to track down a lost child or injured climber. US law enforcement agencies have been and still use these skills to track fugitives and drug traffickers. And the US Border Patrol has highly distinguished itself through its effective use of these techniques in locating and preventing smugglers, illegal immigrants, and all manner of criminals from crossing our borders.

Many developing countries—where modern technology hasn't reached into every corner of society—still depend upon their knowledge of tracking for everyday survival. In fact, many of the skills I will be sharing in this book I learned firsthand from headhunters, bushmen, and native Trackers located throughout the world.

My intention is to bring back an art that has been all but lost from US society, to preserve the hard-earned and much-coveted knowledge learned through years of study, experience, and dedication. My hope is that this knowledge will bring about a safer world; that it will provide skills enabling the average person to better find a lost loved one; and that it will be passed on to succeeding generations before it is lost forever.

With some adaptation, this book can be used anywhere in the world. Unlike other books on tracking, this book focuses on tracking human beings, whether they are enemy soldiers behind our lines, criminals on the run, or children lost in the woods. It is, therefore, intended for use by military personnel, law enforcement officers, and search and rescue teams, although its use is not restricted to public servants. Scouting and adventure groups may find this information helpful for outdoor and survival training; those who have lost their ancient arts may find a connection with their ancestors through the teachings in this book; and any individual who has an interest in this subject can learn a great deal by studying these pages.

What this book will not do is make the reader an expert Tracker. No book alone can do that. It is intended only to cover the fundamentals of ground tracking. To become merely proficient takes time, dedication, and hands-on training under the watchful eye of a skilled and proven Tracker. It takes years of experience and practice—sometimes an entire lifetime—to gain respect as a well-known, accomplished Tracker. But what this book will do is open your eyes to the world around you and move you beyond the level of the beginner and into the ranks of the craftsman.

Welcome and embrace it; tracking is as essential today as it was yesterday, and as it will be tomorrow. Come join the twenty-first-century Tracker as we explore the fundamentals of the past in *Tracking Humans*, and step into the ranks of those who have earned the title of "Tracker."

CHAPTER 1

History and Brief Overview

We and our ancestors are the same . . .
—CARLETON COON

The art of tracking has been around since the creation of humankind and has come full circle with a renewed interest in this nearly extinct science. As important as the advent of farming and the discovery of fire, tracking—and its close cousin, hunting—has been critical to human survival, not only in securing food and clothing, but also in finding shelter from harsh and unforgiving weather, animals, and terrain.

Unfortunately, humans were not equipped with many of the natural abilities of their lower-classed counterparts: They could not run as fast as a cheetah, soar the heavens like an eagle, master the ocean depths like a shark, or crawl up the sides of a cliff like an insect, lizard, or spider; they were not supplied with the keen hearing of a bat, the sharp eyesight of a hawk, the precise homing instinct of a pigeon, nor the discriminating olfactory senses of a dog. Even when it came to catching his prey, humans were left with few natural abilities. Without claws or webs to catch prey, humans had to rely on traps and nets; without sharp teeth or brute strength, humans had to develop the means to kill with club, spear, or arrow; without natural camouflage, humans had to develop techniques to blend in with their surroundings. Humans had to use their superior intelligence to enhance those senses and abilities naturally endowed to their animal counterparts, and they had to develop the means to do this as a group, a pair, or—most critical to their survival—single-handedly.

A SHORT HISTORY

The science of tracking, I'm sure, began when early humans discovered they were hungry and had to find an animal in order to kill and eat it. Since most animals didn't just stand around waiting for the spear or club, humans had to learn how to find their prey. Through trial and error—and the loss of many lives—tracking was developed and fine-tuned over the centuries. Families, tribes, and even entire colonies came to depend on the Tracker's skill for their very survival and control over their domain.[2] Prehistoric art tells countless stories of hunters and their bravery, recounting entire hunts from departure to final victory.

As humankind grew into societies and civilizations, tracking was expanded to include uses outside the basic necessities of life. The ancient Chinese and Japanese used it to wage war against their enemies. Sun Tzu described the importance of using local natives who knew the lay of the land in order to secure victory in a strange territory.[3] This is similar to what the United States recently did in Afghanistan, working closely with the indigenous Northern Alliance to secure victory in that country. Ninja and samurai warriors also had to know these techniques to infiltrate the heart of their enemies' lands.[4] Biblical stories tell of ancient leaders, spies, and undeserving fugitives whose knowledge of the wilderness, its dangers, and its food and water sources ensured the survival of the Israelites. And surely, great warring nations like Rome, Babylon, Chaldea, and Persia, as well as renowned warriors under Alexander the Great, had superior tracking knowledge to so thoroughly and completely defeat their enemies.

During the birth of the American Colonies, Native Americans were instrumental in teaching the colonists ancient arts, which helped their survival. The War of Independence was the first recorded instance of "Europeans" utilizing guerrilla tactics—which the Colonial Army learned from the native tribes. Survival and tracking skills helped give rise to American legends like Daniel Boone, Davy Crockett, and Lewis and

2 Robert Ardrey, *Territorial Imperative* (New York: Atheneum, 1966).

3 Sun Tsu, translated by Samuel B. Griffith, *Sun Tsu, the Art of War, Manoeuver and Employment of Secret Agents,* ed. United Nations Educational, Scientific and Cultural Organization (Oxford: Oxford University Press, 1963): 105, 144–49.

4 Oscar Ratti, Adele Westbrook, *Secrets of the Samurai, Outer Factors of Bijutsu, Ninjitsu* (Rutland, VT: Charles E. Tuttle Co.): 324–31.

Clark, who used their talents to discover new lands and rescue kidnapped women and children.

The nineteenth century saw even greater use of these capabilities. Although slave traders and owners applied these skills to track down escaped slaves, it was the famed Native American scouts who snared the wonder and imagination of generations to come. They used their knowledge and expertise to infiltrate enemy territories, trail renegade Native American bands, and track down famous outlaws to bring them to justice.[5]

Many writings of frontiersmen and soldiers attested to the capabilities of these scouts. One memoir, written by US Army officer Homer Wheeler, captured the skill of one such scout named Poor Elk, trailing renegade Cheyennes near Yellowstone in 1874.

> *Poor Elk followed about a mile to where the pursued party had camped. He brushed away the ashes from the dead fires and felt of the earth underneath, examined the droppings of the animals, counted the number of fires and noticed, by marks made by the pins, the size of the lodges; carefully scrutinized some moccasins, bits of cloth, etc. that had been thrown away; noticed that the moccasins were sewn with thread instead of sinew and were made as the Sioux made them. . . . A sweat-lodge had been built, indicating that they had remained in camp at least one day, and the droppings of the animals determined that the stay had been but one.*
>
> *The position of the camp, the tying of the animals near the tepees and the wickiups, the number of lodges, the care taken by the Indians in leaving, all these things furnished evidence as to the number of Indians and animals and the number of days since they had camped there. Though moving steadily, yet they were in no special hurry; were Sioux and not Cheyennes; had recently left an agency; had not crossed the Yellowstone at the time reported, but two days earlier; were evidently a party of Sioux who were on the way to join the Indians north of the British line. In fact, the record left by these Indians was as complete as though it had been carefully written out.*[6]

5 Gordon C. Baldwin, *The Apache Indian Raiders of the Southwest* (New York: Four Winds, 1978).

6 The Soldiers, *The Old West Series* (New York: Time-Life Books, 1974): 117.

These warriors were trained from their earliest childhoods in the craft of trailing and sign reading, incorporating these skills into every facet of their lives. "Amazing deductions from such sign reading are recorded, and would have seemed impossible if they were not so routinely faced and solved," observes historian Thomas E. Mails.[7]

In the twentieth century, too, as part of law enforcement, military operations, and search and rescue missions, tracking proved its usefulness time and again.

In the early 1950s, Kenyan Mau Maus advocated open revolt against Great Britain. When this took the form of a terrorist campaign aimed at English settlers, the British government hired native Kikuyu Trackers to locate and root out the isolated bands of rebels.[8]

During and after the 1967 Six-Day War, elite Israeli forces, known as Sayeret Scouts, tracked and captured those who sought to destroy the nation of Israel. Today, they are still tracking Palestinian terrorists, smugglers, thieves, and Egyptian spies.[9]

The Vietnam War was the first military conflict that saw extensive use of Special Operations Forces. Between 1964 and 1971, the Studies and Observation Group (SOG), the Vietnam War's covert special warfare unit, fought with distinction and valor, excelling in rescue attempts behind enemy lines, cross-border operations, and reconnaissance missions. Highly skilled in tracking, anti-tracking, and counter-tracking techniques, the SOG owed the success of its Laotian campaign to modern Trackers like Command Sergeant Major Franklin Miller, who learned his craft from the indigenous Montagnards and was awarded the Congressional Medal of Honor for his endeavors.[10]

Even the US Border Patrol can credit many of its achievements to modern-day Trackers. Albert "Ab" Taylor distinguished himself for more than 40 years as the Border Patrol's premier Tracker, discovering and

7 *The Mystic Warriors of the Plains* (New York: Marlowe & Company, 1995): 523.

8 Robert B. Edgerton, *Mau Mau: An African Crucible* (New York: Ballatine Books, 1989).

9 Moshe Betser and Robert Rosenberg, *Secret Soldier* (New York: Atlantic Monthly Press, 1996).

10 John L. Plaster, *SOG: The Secret Wars of America's Commandos in Vietnam* (New York: Simon & Schuster, 1997).

preventing scores of drug traffickers from entering the country as well as participating in countless search and rescue missions.[11]

Included among the remarkable Trackers of our time is one who uses tracking in a unique way. Instead of utilizing his skills to harm or capture humans, Sydney Possuelo tracks people to preserve them. He travels the jungles of Brazil along the Amazon River to locate and thereafter protect the indigenous people of South America, in an effort to preserve their culture from modern intrusions for generations to come.[12]

The twenty-first-century world-famous Trackers have yet to be discovered. They could include a quiet, unassuming Special Operations soldier, a Crocodile Dundee–like character discovered by a zealous newspaper columnist in the Australian outback, or someone who is just now learning the art of tracking—someone such as you.

A TRACKING OVERVIEW

But what does it really take to be a modern Tracker? As I'm sure you've guessed, it requires more than just the techniques written in this book.

First, it takes physical stamina. Whatever your role, be it as an elite ground force soldier or search and rescue team member, you must be able to outlast your Chase. You must be physically fit, capable of walking ten, fifty, one hundred miles over steep and rugged terrain, traveling for days on nothing but your own two feet with a forty- to ninety-pound pack on your back. You must have the ability to carry or find your own food and water, and to pack whatever equipment you need for survival. And you must be able to do this while protecting yourself from all possible dangers.

While I am not a certified physical trainer, I do know a little bit about building both strength and endurance after twenty years in Special Operations units. To put it simply, running, biking, swimming, hiking, and skipping rope are all good cardiovascular exercises to build your stamina and long-distance endurance, and you should practice your exercise(s) of choice at least three to four times weekly. Weight lifting, push-ups,

11 Donald C. Cooper and Albert "Ab" Taylor, *The Fundamentals of Mantracking* (Olympia, WA: Emergency Response Institute and National Rescue Consultants, 1990).

12 Sydney Possuelo, "Hidden Tribes of the Amazon," *National Geographic* (August 2003): 2–27.

sit-ups, knee-bends, dips, chin-ups, and pull-ups are all good strength-building exercises and should also be done three to four times per week. If you would like more in-depth knowledge on this subject, please consult your local gym or personal trainer.

The next skill you need is an excessive amount of attention to detail. You must be able to perceive more than the average person; you must be able to "see" everything presented before you, whether visible or not. One missed sign could send you off track for a hundred square miles and could mean the difference between life and death—either the Chase's or your own. And you must have a good memory to recall what you have discovered, since pencils, tablets, and cameras may not always be available.

Also you need the appropriate tools.

As with any extended trip into the woods, mountains, or desert, a compass is an absolute necessity, as are appropriate maps of the area, which can be obtained from the US Geological Survey or most outdoor recreation equipment outlets.

You will need survival gear appropriate for the climate, weather, and terrain conditions. For winter weather, this obviously means warm and layered clothing, head and hand protection, nonslip boots, skis or snow-shoes, dry socks, and sturdy shelter. For hot weather, this could mean jungle boots, a floppy hat with plenty of aeration, light clothing, mosquito netting, or hammock materials. All facets of self-protection and survival must be taken into consideration.

In order to record your findings, you will need writing tools, a tablet, a tape recorder, a camera and/or camcorder, and the appropriate type and number of batteries to operate them. To gather evidence, you will need plastic or ziplock bags, a digging tool, tweezers, and gloves. Some Trackers have even found a magnifying glass helpful in their searches and for their own survival.

Merging this ancient skill with modern technology has been and continues to be quite an eye-opener. Palantir, Query Tree, and Analyst Notebook are excellent software tools to efficiently and quickly distribute the immediate details gathered by a person with tracking skills. These applications can immediately distribute intelligence in real time across a large spectrum within the area of operation or interest. This information comes in handy to ensure the survival of friendly and innocent missing persons as well as in capturing insurgents, guerrillas, or fugitives from the law. The software complements the efforts of a skillful human Trackers who can gather immediate information from an incident site, such as a single tire print or footprint evidence at a crime scene, by collating each bit of tactical intelligence and making it available to any personnel involved in the investigation. Many of these software tools are being used in federal domestic security as well as the military.

Finally, you will require enough food and water (including a water-purification system or tablets) to last at least the expected duration of the search or until you can be resupplied. As a precaution, if resupply is unlikely or unattainable, it may be appropriate to pack enough supplies to last as long as two days beyond the anticipated time frame, if you have the space and can carry the weight. Just a quick note: Since Vitamin A enhances natural night vision, try to pack foods or supplements that contain it to give yourself the best possible advantage during hours of darkness.

A few safety tips may be in order here. Wear some sort of eye protection, such as sunglasses or safety glasses, even if you have perfect eyesight. I have seen too many cases of people needing hospitalization because of an unseen twig, branch, or dangerous chemical injuring their eyes. If you have eyesight correctable through contact lenses or glasses, always carry a spare set of either or both; gas mask optical inserts are a must. If you depend on glasses, bring along antifog drops or spray, since glasses tend to fog up with very little effort on your part; additionally, antiglare, antifog, and scratch-resistant glasses with UV protection are now on the market and sold to the general public. Those looking for more permanent eyesight corrections might seek the advice of their eye doctor concerning laser surgery.

If you will be exposed to loud noises, such as those from explosives, aircraft, or weapons, use hearing protection during training. Fitted or spongy earplugs are best, but I have been known to use tissue or wadded-up toilet paper when nothing else was available. Chances are that you are going to survive the ordeal. If not, you will be no worse off for wearing the ear protection; if so, you will be glad you took the extra precaution.

If afforded such luxury, by all means use binoculars, spotting scopes, night vision goggles or sights, and thermal imaging devices. Just remember that there is a downside to these in a hostile environment: Optics often cause a reflection that could quickly expose your location. (Note: As a good anti-tracking technique, place nylon or panty hose fabric over the optic to eliminate 95 percent of the reflection while allowing nearly unimpeded vision; there are also commercial "anti-reflex" devices that can be placed over the optics.)

While smoking or not smoking is a personal decision, there are a couple of things you need to keep in mind. First, nonsmokers have a keener sense of smell. If you want to be an effective Tracker, all of your senses must be operating at their peaks. Second, cigarette smoke is one of the quickest ways to compromise your position in a hostile environment. If you must smoke, do it at the base camp; on the trail, refrain from it for the safety of your team members. Ask your physician about nicotine patches, gum, or other smoking withdrawal aids.

Whatever you do, take the time to gather the appropriate gear. The success of your search may well depend upon selecting the right equipment for the task at hand.

Once you have completed this crucial step, you are ready to embark on your tracking adventure. The following pages will be filled with instructions, photos, and true-to-life illustrations of a chase in progress. Some of the lessons will be easy to visualize; others will require practical and hands-on study to fully understand the applicable instruction. I hope to empower you with the ability to look beyond the obvious in order to read the full story as told by various signs before you.

Good luck, and I'll see you at the end of the trail!

"PREY-LUDE" TO THE CHASE

Near the border between the two Koreas, just south of the Demilitarized Zone (DMZ), members of US Army Special Forces Operational Detachment 266 huddle together in a cigar-shaped perimeter. They sit shoulder to shoulder in a secured sleep site during a combined nation training exercise involving both US and Republic of Korea (ROK) military forces.[13] Over the past two weeks, they have proven their skills in unconventional warfare tactics to the observer-controllers overseeing the exercise. Their team alone has surprised and "neutralized" two teams of mock North Korean Opposing Forces (OPFOR), just in the past three days. Now, nearing the end of the exercise, all team members are anxious for the "END-EX" announcement. Weapons sergeant Francisco ("Frank") Badilla and radio operator Bob Rowe discuss in hushed tones a strange message that has just come over the radio.

300245LMAR02 (30 March 2002, 2:45 a.m. Local) THIS IS NOT AN EXERCISE. THIS IS NOT AN EXERCISE. BE PREPARED FOR LIVE MISSION. EXECUTION ORDER HAND CARRIED BY MAJOR KIM CHONG HEE, ATTACHED TO TEAM AS ADVISOR AND INTERPRETER. EMERGENCY RESUPPLY BUNDLES TO BE AIRLIFTED TO YOUR POSITION VIA HUEY. ANY REQUIRED EQUIPMENT MUST BE REQUESTED WITHIN 30 MINUTES. PRE-POSITION UNNEEDED EQUIPMENT FOR HUEY PICKUP.

"Live mission. Right," says Rowe sarcastically. "They probably want us to *think* that. Just like last time they pulled that on us."

"Yeah, maybe," agrees Badilla. "But we still need to report this."

Paul O'Connor, the team medic, crawls up beside them, touching their arms and signaling them to be quiet. He points to a ridge on their left, where the bright moonlight silhouettes four human figures against the skyline. The figures are moving eastward and appear to be carrying the distinctive-looking AK-47 rifles of the North Korean armies.

"They've got to be OPFOR," O'Connor declares.

---

13 Although based in South Korea, the scenario, events, geographic locations, and people used in this illustration are fictional. Any similarities to real-life operations are purely coincidental.

"We'd better tell Samoa," Badilla says. "We may have another OPFOR team to knock off."

Badilla quietly approaches their team leader, a large master sergeant from the island of Samoa. "Radio transmission just came in," he says, handing the Samoan the transcribed piece of paper. "Something about a live mission and resupply bundles being airlifted to our position."

Samoa reads the transmission, his expression serious.

"Oh, by the way," Badilla continues, "I think some OPFOR passed by on the ridge about ten minutes ago. They looked like they were carrying AK-47s."

Samoa turns his head toward Badilla, a frown darkening his face. "There are no ROK or US OPFOR working in this area. And AK-47s are used by the North Korean People's Army—our OPFOR teams don't have any. As soon as those emergency bundles arrive, I want you and O'Connor to check out who the heck *did* pass by the ridge earlier."

By this time, the rest of the team members are wide-awake, sensing the urgency of the situation. Samoa looks around at the gathering group of men. "Better get your gear packed up and ready to move out. Looks like we're going into action."

In the night sky, dark and thick with fog, two Huey helicopters soon announce their coming, their distinctive *whump, whump, whump* muffled as they approach from the northwest at treetop level. The choppers hover over the makeshift drop zone one foot above the tree line, one hoisting down the emergency resupply bundle while the other simultaneously drops a fastrope to allow a Korean passenger to slide to the ground. The visiting team evaluator and unneeded equipment are lifted up and quickly removed from the area of operations.

Samoa approaches the Korean officer, extending his hand. "Welcome, sir. I am Malupa Tumera. My men call me Samoa."

The Korean officer returns the handshake with a smile. "Hello, I am Major Kim Chong Hee from the Republic of Korea Army. You got our message?"

Samoa nods. "Yes, sir. I don't suppose this has anything to do with the four people we saw earlier this morning, carrying AK-47s?"

Major Kim straightens quickly. "You saw them? Here?"

"Yes, sir. About two hours ago."

"Did you see which way they traveled?"

"It was dark, but they appeared to be heading eastward."

Major Kim looks around at the tired but steely-eyed Green Berets standing near him. "I understand you are the best. They say you track anyone. Is this correct?"

The Samoan nods with confidence. "Sir, just tell us when to start."

CHAPTER 2

Getting to Know You

I keep six honest serving men
(They taught me all I knew):
Their names are What and Why and When
And How and Where and Who

—RUDYARD KIPLING

Our quarry in this book is known by many titles, depending on the agency using the terms. In law enforcement circles, this individual is known as the "suspect" or "fugitive," sheriffs of the Old West named them "outlaws," and bounty hunters today refer to this person in all sorts of unprintable terms. Intelligence organizations chase "rabbits." In search and rescue operations, the individual sought is known as the "victim." Hunters use the term "quarry," while the big game itself may see the hunters as *its* "prey." Regardless of the semantics, I will refer to this particular individual as the "Chase," defined by *Webster's* as "one being chased." This word, I believe, is the most appropriate term for this book because it covers nearly every possible characteristic of the person being sought.

So who is this Chase? What does he look like? How will we know him when we find him? Or more important, how do we know *how* to find him?

Since human beings are creatures of habit, our familiarization with the Chase's habits will enable us, the Trackers, to easily begin and maintain the pursuit of this individual. Knowledge in this case is true power. Every possible detail must be explored and weighed for relevance. The more knowledgeable we are about our Chase's physical characteristics as well as his peculiarities, the better chance we have of using that information to our advantage. Knowing, for example, that a child lost in the woods always wears Nike shoes could lead you straight to her just by following the unique imprints in the dirt and/or low-level "top signs" because of her height. Armed with information that your Chase is a militant infiltrator highly skilled in designing booby traps, you could alert your team to such, preventing any of you from stumbling blindly into a concealed bomb or trip wire.

It is extremely important that we absorb a great deal of information as quickly as possible. Delays in gathering this information could mean the disappearance of valuable traces and signs and the waste of precious minutes, hours, or days. Sometimes, the collection of facts must be weighed against the possible loss of critical physical details, and sometimes this judgment call must be made in a matter of minutes.

So, where do you get such information? It depends on why you need it and how much time you have.

The obvious place to start is with those closest to you. In military units, that means debriefing and accumulating reports from previous patrols, tracker teams, reconnaissance teams, intelligence organizations at all levels, native peoples, prisoners of war, and civilian authorities. To those in law enforcement, it means searching the national crime databases or the Department of Motor Vehicles and conferring with undercover agents and informants with possible knowledge of the Chase. Search and rescue teams understand the importance of consulting with the Chase's family members, friends, coworkers, witnesses, or camping buddies. Natives, people living in the area in which he was last seen, and anyone else with possible knowledge of the victim can also be good sources of information. Other possible sources include private investigators, the local library, and the National Center for Missing and Exploited Children (their website is www.missingkids.com, and their twenty-four-hour toll-free hotline is 800-843-5678). And if you have Internet resources available, by all means use them!

Once you know where to go, what information do you need? Absolutely everything you can get, from his favorite color to the name of his dog! Don't forget his birthday (or his children's birthdays), his family's address, and information about his close friends. If family members are in the hospital, determine which hospital and the estimated length of stay. These significant dates, times, and places may lead you right to your Chase. Obtain clear evidence as well as mere hints about his lifestyle.

Although it may seem elementary, what are his physical characteristics, such as height, weight, skin color, hair color, eyes, nationality? Is the Chase a male, female, homosexual, or bisexual? Does he cross-dress? Is one leg longer than the other, thereby causing him to walk with a limp or a cane? Does he have distinctive body marks, such as birthmarks, lacerations, scars, or tattoos? What was he wearing when he was last seen? There is an old but true adage that says, "A picture paints a thousand words." Obtain a recent photograph and then imagine the difference if the Chase has grown a beard or mustache, shaved his head, or is wearing glasses or contacts. Is he on foot or in a vehicle? (See appendix A, "Human Profile Card," and appendix B, "Vehicle Profile Card.")

What does he like to eat? Are there ethnic dishes he is most likely to consume? What are the most common foods he eats on a daily basis? Is he a vegetarian, meat-and-potatoes fanatic, or junk food lover? Does he consume a lot, or does he eat only what he absolutely needs to survive?

What is his medical history? Find out if he has any injuries, medical problems or conditions, allergies, intolerance to heat or cold, or anything that you can use to your advantage. Does he require the regular use of prescription drugs? Is he asthmatic, needing inhalants for his condition? If he is diabetic, does he use insulin or take medication? Does he wear glasses, contacts, a hearing aid, false teeth, or a wig? What color or style are they?

What are his daily, weekly, monthly routines and hygienic habits, including flossing and brushing his teeth? Does he perform religious or other rituals? What kind of habits does he have (smoking cigarettes, biting fingernails, chewing gum or tobacco, taking illegal drugs) that may leave residue or implements of some kind, giving clues to his whereabouts? Is he a heavy caffeine drinker, undergoing severe caffeine withdrawal and the associated headaches? Does he lay on his back when he sleeps?

Don't forget to inquire about his mental abilities. Is he an adult or child? Is his mind stable? Does he get easily frustrated or angry, causing interference with his reasoning skills? Is he learning disabled? Does he have Alzheimer's?

Habitat is also key to getting a full picture of and thoroughly understanding the Chase. Knowing the environment he is accustomed to and/ or familiar with will tell you his capabilities in the present environment.

What is his current residence or his last-known address? In what type of area is he comfortable? Obviously, if he is a "city slicker" who has known only urban or suburban life, he is going to be at a great disadvantage in the midst of a national forest. If he is a recluse, used to living by himself in a mountain cabin, he will probably have a better chance of tolerating the wilderness and eluding his pursuers. Those living in rural or country settings may be accustomed to killing and eating wild animals to survive; those living in or on the streets of the city may be accustomed to scrounging, hustling, stealing, or fighting others for their next meal. Regardless of the environment, any one of these people may have the potential to kill others—especially those they feel are a threat to their survival or well-being.

What about the Chase's life philosophies? Does he regularly observe ethnic or personal customs? What traditions did he grow up with and still holds on to today? What are his political beliefs and viewpoints? What type of training did he have? Is he a member of a terrorist group? If so, which group, and what do they believe in? Are they likely to use rifles to advance their cause, or are they more likely to make a statement with explosives or booby traps? Is the Chase a survivalist, a white supremacist? Who trained him? What are his likely courses of action if pushed or trapped? How does his religious faith influence his actions? Will he kill in order to ensure his entrance into "heaven" or seek peace at all cost? Has he aligned himself or sworn loyalty/allegiance to cults, terrorists, or Mafia-type organizations? A loyal disciple can be so devoted to a cause that he, without conscience, is willing to kill or die for it, blatantly disregarding all reputable law. (Warning: Leave such matters to the proper authorities!)

The answer to all of these questions, and more, may mean the difference between success and failure. It may also mean the difference between life and death when coming face-to-face with a desperate fugitive or enemy insurgent. Learn all you can about your Chase, as quickly as you can, in order to make intelligent deductions and decisions, both before and during your pursuit. Due to time constraints or limited resources, gathering such information may be lessons in futility. In those cases, use your best judgment on the information you can't get. Take what you've got, hope that it's enough, and request updated information while on the move.

Just remember, the clock is ticking, daylight is limited, and time cannot be turned back. Take the initiative and go!

OPERATION CHASE

Badilla and O'Connor scramble to secure their gear from the emergency bundle, as the rest of the group follows Major Kim to see the detachment commander, a warrant officer the team addresses simply as "Jordan." After the formalities and introductions, Radio operator Rowe, who is also the recorder, pulls out a waterproof tablet and pencil from his BDU pockets. Major Kim speaks to the gathered team members, describing the incidents and the intelligence reports gathered thus far.

•••

On 27 March, in the territorial waters of the Japanese Sea, three miles south and four miles east of the DMZ along the South Korean coast, a Republic of Korea warship seized a midget submarine (1st Incident of the Infiltration). Intelligence files indicated that similar submersibles had been used primarily to transport infiltrator spies or insurgents who had caused deadly harm and havoc to local communities. They had also been used to conduct coastal surveillance.

The warship was towing the submersible to the nearby port along the Kangwon Province, in order to pry open the hatch. Along the way, the submarine sank; the fate of the crew was unknown.

After the submarine was recovered on 28 March, the hatch was explosively breached, and it was discovered that there was but one person inside the watercraft, found dead. The death had been caused by cyanide poisoning (2nd Incident of the Infiltration). The discovery of only one person caused instant alarm, triggering the plan for an immediate and extensive search; normally, there would be four or five people aboard such submersibles.

The morning of 28 March, a corpse was found in a shallow grave by a curious dog digging in the fresh dirt (3rd Incident of the Infiltration); the body was located ten miles from the coast in a draw near the small town of Kansong. The unknown victim was of Korean descent, with Adidas-brand clothing, military-style boots, and a bullet wound at the base of the head. His left hand displayed an unusual blister, which immediately prompted the airlift of a pathologist/communicable disease expert, along with a forensic ballistics expert and an intelligence officer, to the third incident location.

The ballistics expert concluded that the round at the base of the head had been fired by a 7.62 Type 64 pistol, shot at close range. This type of pistol, specifically of the silencer variety, was known to be carried by North Korean infiltrators.

The intelligence officer indicated that the Adidas clothing worn by the victim was similar to that found on three infiltrators killed four months earlier on 9 November while attempting to cross over into South Korea.

The pathologist/communicable disease expert used his portable field lab to confirm the fears that prompted his arrival. The fluid-filled blister, surrounded by swelling at the site of infection, characterized skin exposure to a form of anthrax. [Anthrax—or *Bacillus anthracis*—is a bacterial, zoological disease that can be easily mass-produced on a small budget with low overhead. The bacterium is odorless and microscopic, unable to be seen with the naked eye; its delivery is noiseless unless combined with an explosive such as a bomb or mortar. Anthrax, and its resulting disease, falls into the category of one of the top stealth killers of humanity.]

On the morning of 29 March, fifteen miles east of Detachment 266, a local farmer gathering mushrooms was reported missing. Local inhabitants reported that "the dogs were going crazy" that morning (4th Incident of the Infiltration).

Based on these four incidents, the close proximity of the detachment to the last known incident, and the detachment's reputation for expert tracking, Operational Detachment 266 was brought into the manhunt. The Republic of Korea asked this Special Forces team, along with a Korean representative, to terminate the intent of the infiltrators.

The Korean government did not want the infiltrators spooked. With the enemy's close proximity to the long Tae 'Baek mountain range, they could easily evade a massive manhunt in the numerous hills and ridges which proliferated and crisscrossed in every direction. The fact that they could be carrying biological weapons was further cause for concern since they could activate the contaminants, which could possibly include cholera, in any water source they pleased if they felt compromise was imminent.

The US National Command Authority was in agreement with the South Korean government to allow the infiltrators to believe they had successfully and without compromise infiltrated the area, so that they would not be forced into an irrational decision. Higher headquarters believed the team could, with stealth, bring on the surprise capture or, if need be, the elimination of these infiltrators, thereby preventing a biological disaster.

•••

"Okay, gentlemen," Jordan addresses the team, summing up the information. "You've got the picture. It has been confirmed that all our OPFOR have been out of the exercise box for the past twenty-four hours. Therefore, what we saw this morning was four suspected North Korean infiltrators passing by on the ridge, carrying AK-47s. You've just been told that they also have Type 64 pistols, possibly with silencers, which they have already used on one of their own—probably a defector. They may be wearing Adidas clothing, military clothing, or a combination of both; and they may have a hostage with them. If spooked, they could contaminate the water in the whole friggin' countryside." He passes his eyes along the assembled group. "The last two weeks were just practice. These guys are for real. Let's be efficient; let's be careful; but let's go get 'em!"

CHAPTER 3

My Common Senses Will Find You

In the act of hunting, a man becomes, however briefly, part of nature again. He returns to the natural state, becomes one with the animal, and is freed of the existential split: to be part of nature and to transcend it by virtue of his consciousness.

—Erich Fromm

An astute Tracker must be able to locate, identify, and pursue "signs," which can be anything altered from its natural state. Pertinent signs are those inflicted on a single geographic location or object by means of the Chase's body or his associated equipment. By combining these with intelligence and deductive reasoning, we will gain sensible and accurate information about the Chase. Signs left behind, however, are not always apparent to the naked eye. The Tracker, therefore, must use all senses to identify signs masked by time, weather, or the Chase himself.

Many of our senses have become deadened, suffering from lack of use, misuse, or self-abuse, and the purpose of this chapter is to encourage their revitalization. The reason is simple. Without access to sophisticated scopes and electronic devices, our senses may be the only means available to obtain clues of the Chase's whereabouts. Ancient humans, hunters, and natives of yesterday possessed finely honed senses, sharpened by their constant use and continuous training. In order to attain similar tracking expertise, we must do the same.

Trackers use four of their senses to identify signs: sight, hearing, smell, and touch, with a good dose of the sixth sense—intuition—thrown in when the others have been exhausted or diminished. And unless you are a Canadian Mountie named Benton Frazier from the Northwest Territory, we'll leave taste to those schooled in its usage.[14] Of course, proper use of these physical tools requires not only intellect, but also optimum health, if they are to be exerted to their full potential. All factors—senses, intellect, and deductive reasoning—are of equal importance for the expeditious recovery of your Chase.

SIGHT

Sight is the most commonly used of all senses for those of us blessed with natural or corrected 20/20 vision. But for the purpose of tracking, even sight needs to be broken down into different categories for specific purposes.

Visual Tracking

Visual tracking is the ability to identify marks and signs left by your Chase. Without a doubt, this is the primary means by which Trackers gather information.

Before we get into the specifics of using sight, let me offer a simple explanation from David LeVay's *Human Anatomy and Physiology* of how the eye "sees," so that you can better understand the principles of night vision through adaptation and application.

> *The cup-shaped retina has two different systems of receptors: rods and cones. The rods, with their visual purple, are for blacks, whites, and greys under twilight conditions. The cones have other pigments for colour vision in bright light; when this system is defective, the individual is colour-blind. In darkness the retina becomes more sensitive to the available light, the phenomenon of adaptation.*[15]

14 George Bloomfield, prod., *Due South,* Alliance Atlantis Communications, CBS/CTV, 1997–1998.

15 *Human Anatomy and Physiology* (Lincolnwood, IL: Contemporary Books, 2001): 359.

It takes the human eye thirty minutes to adapt to the night. Most people experience this phenomenon when entering a darkened movie theater.

Adaptation to Darkness. As previously stated, the retina, in darkness, becomes receptive to ambient light by producing sufficient visual purple rod cells. The result is the ability to differentiate objects in low light within thirty minutes.

Application: Off-Center Vision. In order to adequately see objects in dark or semidark conditions, you must not look at an object directly, or it will seem to disappear. Looking at objects directly utilizes the cone area of the retina, which is not active during times of darkness. Rather, you must look to the left, right, above, or below an object you are observing in order to most effectively utilize that area of the retina containing the rod cells, which are sensitive in darkness. Continually move your eyes around your target, pausing at various points to ascertain and verify the identity of the target object.

•••

Like an art student learning the specifics of light and shadow, the Tracker must also understand the fine points of visual perception, in order to exploit this sense's natural ability. While I am not a professional painter or photographer, I can present those techniques learned through careful study and my twenty years of experience.

There are six primary factors that make objects visible: shape, shadows, silhouettes, movement, spacing, and surfaces.

Shape. Every object on this planet has a shape unique to itself. A tree is easily distinguished from a factory; a discarded soup can is just as easily differentiated from the short-cropped grass on which it lies. The human body has a very definitive shape, as does equipment associated with certain vocations or professions, and both can be recognized precisely when compared with their surroundings.

Unless specifically concealed, distinctive shapes can be seen instantly. A soldier in the field, for example, can be easily recognized by his Kevlar helmet, M-16 rifle, backpack, or equipment belt loaded with ammo pouches, canteens, and first-aid kits. A well-camouflaged soldier, on the other hand, blends in with his surroundings, eliminating the unique shapes that can expose him to enemy fire.

Shadows. These can be placed in two categories: cast and contained.

Cast shadows are those extending from still, moving, or suspended objects or substances, due to some form of illumination from the opposite side. These types of shadows are caused by either artificial light, such as that from a flashlight, streetlight, or headlight, or natural light from the sun or moon. In some cases, they can be caused by other natural sources like the aurora borealis, or northern lights, in Canada or Alaska. Even stationary objects can be compromised through the rotation of the sun or moon. What is well hidden in the morning can be widely exposed by noon and casting a long shadow by early evening. In a similar manner, differing seasons can expose and illuminate that which was safely in the shadows earlier in the year.

Contained shadows, on the other hand, are just that, contained within a body or cavity, such as a cave or darkened room. They can be easily distinguished from other types of shadows, since they are normally darker, larger, and more uniform than other types of shadows.

Silhouetting. A silhouette occurs when a light object is contrasted against a dark surface, such as an individual in white snow gear walking along the edge of a forest. It also occurs when a dark object can be distinguished from a light background, such as a person standing or walking along a ridgeline in the full moonlight.

Movement. Moving objects have always been known to attract attention. In fact, many species in the animal kingdom have been programmed to initiate a heated chase after the sudden movement of prospective prey. Even with its keen eyesight, an eagle cannot locate a field mouse that is sitting quietly in a field, openly exposed. Let that same mouse skitter across a small patch of ground, and it quickly becomes the predator's dinner. People living on the outskirts of wilderness areas are often warned not to run from a bear or mountain lion, since this often provokes the animal to pursue what it perceives as prey. Just watch a house cat follow this same pattern. Lying lazily in a patch of sunlight, the cat will doze off, bored with its environment. Jerk a small object on a string, and the same cat is upright and alert in a split second, clawing and playing with the moving item.

People have also been programmed with this same ability. A well-camouflaged person is extremely hard to identify; but let him move in an obvious way (like standing up), and he becomes target practice for any sniper. As Trackers, we can also use this as a means of locating our Chase. In a still, quiet early morning, the slightest movement can attract our attention. It may be the Chase himself, extricating himself from his sleeping area, or it may be a rope, piece of cloth, or antenna wire inadvertently left swinging from a tree limb.

Spacing. The spacing of objects is often overlooked by the amateur Tracker, and it is rarely if ever considered by those who regularly hunt big game or fowl. Natural objects are rarely systematically placed. Humans, as creatures of habit and orderliness, are the only known creatures that purposefully line up objects. Hence, orchards and cornfields are precisely laid out, with perfectly straight rows that crisscross evenly in every geometric direction. In the military, where "dress right dress" is a way of life, even individual fighting positions are evenly spaced across a line of fire, in order to prevent exposing sectors of weakness to an attacking enemy. Therefore, when approaching small hills or bushes lined up systematically across his path, a Tracker should be on the immediate alert for the combatants and weapons that could be hiding behind or within them.

Surface. Differences in surface should also catch the Tracker's attention. If the face and texture of an object differ from its surroundings, it will be plainly exposed and subject to closer scrutiny. An old and rough split-rail fence post would not normally cause alarm or attract attention. But a bright scratch against the graying wood certainly calls for a closer look.

Scanning and Searching

Once you know the six factors that make objects visible, you will be able to see those objects, which may be surrounded by a sea of green vegetation. In order to effectively pick out those objects, there are two methods I use to systematically search an entire geographic area.

Scanning. Scanning is a methodical and general overview of an area. It does not involve an in-depth search, at least not initially. The purpose is to sweep a large area entirely, ensuring that your whole viewpoint has been exposed to your eyes.

To effectively scan an area, divide the area horizontally into thirds. Imagine the territory in front of you is a two-dimensional canvas of a painted nature scene. The top boundary is the horizon; the bottom boundary is the ground in front of you. Now divide that canvas into three equal parts: the foreground, the mid-distance, and the far ground.

The foreground is the area directly to your front. It can include the dirt beneath you and extends up about a third of the way from your feet to the horizon. Depending upon the type of terrain you are navigating, that distance could be twenty-five feet or a quarter mile. If you are in a heavily wooded area, then twenty-five feet in any direction may make up the entire foreground. In a barren desert, the foreground could cover a quarter mile or more.

The mid-distance is the middle third of the canvas, and again, it could consist of anywhere from twenty-five feet in front of you to a mile or more.

The far ground is the top third and can stretch as far as the eye can see.

In order to "see" everything in such a vast area, it must be scanned systematically. With a horizontal movement of your eyes, sweep the foreground from left to right, right to left, and left to right, moving your line of vision up just enough to slightly overlap the area above the last sweep. In this way, work your way upward to the far ground.

Searching. At any moment during your scan, you can begin to search, which is an in-depth analysis of an area or object. Any *suspected* movement, disturbance, or object should call for an immediate and careful search for signs left by your Chase.

Since you should always have a partner with you, have him or her visually mark and watch the area(s) of disturbance while you continue to scan the remaining ground to ensure there is no immediate threat of danger. If no threat is imminent, go to the closest disturbance first. If a threat is discovered, avoid it if possible; if a threat is identified as your Chase, proceed to that area immediately. I will cover in-depth analysis and search of an area in chapter 4.

AUDITORY TRACKING

Auditory tracking is the ability to identify sounds made directly by humans or indirectly through their activities. And yes, even this can be broken down into further categories, to which I have assigned the values of vocal (direct) and mechanical (indirect) noises.

Vocal Noises

Vocal sounds are those that proceed directly from a person's respiratory system. They are formed by the mouth and convey a message, such as talking, whispering, shouting, screaming, whistling, laughing, and crying. They can also be made up of intentional or unintentional mouth, nasal, and throat reverberations, such as gasps, hiccups, coughs, sneezes, and actions such as spitting, vomiting, and blowing the nose.

Mechanical Noises

Mechanical noises, on the other hand, are those that result from a person's interaction with his body, equipment, other people, animals, foliage, inanimate matter, and other natural objects within his local environment. This category covers the gamut of nearly every other possible sound the Chase could make.

The Chase can interact with his own body by clapping hands, cracking or popping joints, or snapping fingers (as if to music or as a signal). What he can't control is noisy bodily functions such as gurgling hunger pangs, passing gas, and burping.

Contact between a person and his environment could cause the *snap, crunch, splash,* and *squish* made when stepping on dry leaves, twigs, broken glass, gravel, water, and mud. An astute Tracker can distinctly hear a person brushing against low-hanging branches, pulling away from thorns and blackberry bushes, or opening a door or gate.

The Chase's interaction with his own clothing and equipment can also expose him to auditory discovery. He may be doing a mundane thing like pulling up a zipper, unbuckling a strap, lighting a match, pulling loose a Velcro fastener, or removing his backpack. Or he may be throwing caution to the wind by chopping wood, clanging metal on metal, or releasing and slamming the bolt of a weapon in preparation for use.

27

But be on the "hear-out" (as opposed to lookout) for other mechanical, electric, or electronic noises that the Chase may or may not be able to control. The beeping of a digital watch or pager is a good example, as is the ring of a cell phone or the "low battery" signal made by a laptop or portable phone. If the Chase has a radio, listen for the quick beep following the end of a transmission, or the brief second of static before the squelch takes over.

Each person can add to this list, based on his or her own unique life experiences. The next time you are out in the woods, pay attention to how loud it is, especially in the dark or on a cold, crisp morning with no clouds or fog to deaden the vibrations. Even when you are trying to be quiet, the noise often rings clearly in your ears.

Through a combination of sight and sound, you will be able to estimate distance. Sound travels at a speed of 720 miles per hour or 350 meters (1,100 feet) per second. If you suddenly see a bright flash, a puff of smoke, or dust rising, start counting, "One thousand one, one thousand two, one thousand three . . ." until you hear the audible signature from that area. Every one second ("one thousand one") counted, the sound travels 350 meters. Therefore, if you see a flash and start counting, then stop at "one thousand four" when you hear the noise, the distance from the target area to your location will be approximately 1,400 meters, or a just under a mile (as the bird flies).

Although I am no expert on the distance over which sound carries, I do know that at night it carries much farther than in the daylight. This is partially because, at night, less noise is made that can interfere with your normal hearing—at least in an urban setting. In a wooded, forested, or jungle environment, greater numbers of predators and vociferous insects are active at night; therefore, distinguishing between animal and artificial sounds could actually save your life—or at least save you a great deal of embarrassment. The other factors involve atmospheric conditions, including cooler, damper night air. Normally, you can clearly identify and even estimate the direction of the originator, unless the sound is affected by refraction or reflection of some kind.

Any exterior obstacle that blocks or muffles sound waves causes reflection. Some of these obstacles can be animate or inanimate objects, such as trees, rain, hail, running water, and buildings. They can be intangible entities such as wind; thunder; vibrations or rumbling from trains, heavy machinery, and aircraft; or the swoosh of vehicular traffic on a road or highway. Your own team's lack of noise discipline could make it hard to correctly identify and effectively locate critical sounds. On the other hand, your own clothing could work against you. Loud, rubbing cloth such as Gore-Tex, vinyl, or rubber could easily distract you or mask noises made by someone or something else. And protective coverings such as hats, helmets, hoods, earmuffs, or earplugs will most definitely make the job much more difficult.

No matter what geographical area you live in, it is equally important to become familiar with the sounds that indigenous animals, birds, reptiles, or insects make, especially when threatened by a human or natural predator. Familiarity with the animals in their natural habitats allows you to be aware of their state of serenity as well as their distress. They may alert you to the presence of an individual near you; they may just as easily assure you that no one is anywhere close to your position. Dogs bark when alerting to someone who is disturbing the stillness or approaching their territory; they emit a much higher-pitched bark or near-yelp when scared or defending their terrain. Birds may begin to frantically chirp, caw, or hoot to ward off unwanted visitors around their nests. Insects, on the other hand, may grow quiet when approached by a prospective predator.

Differentiating between the myriad tones resonating from all directions will help you to lay aside unproved theories. The more certain you are of the sounds you are hearing, the more conclusive your evidence becomes. The true Tracker knows his surroundings and eliminates much of the guesswork during his fact-finding mission. By reducing the assumptions and guesswork, he can concentrate fully on the facts and the conclusive evidence before him.

Just remember, in the same way that noise can reveal your Chase's whereabouts, it can just as easily betray your position. Whenever possible, be sure to utilize natural or external man-made noises (such as a nearby airplane or artillery barrage) to conceal your own movements.

SCENT TRACKING

When we think of "following a scent," we almost always associate this action with dogs. How do they follow a scent? How do they differentiate between one person and another?

Bill and Jean Syrotuck's extensive research answered most of these questions about airborne scent, which was featured in the American Rescue Dog Association's *Search and Rescue Dogs*.

Humans constantly shed small cornflake-shaped dead skin cells known as rafts, which are discarded at the rate of about 40,000 per minute. Each raft carries bacteria and vapor representing the unique, individual scent of the person. This is the scent sought by the trained dog. These rafts are picked up and carried by air and wind currents. They are dispersed down wind in a conelike shape that is narrow and concentrated at its source (the person), but widening as the distance grows. Trained dogs can be observed literally working the cone in open fields as they zigzag back and forth, in and out of the scent.[16]

Human tracking by smell is very similar to the technique commonly used by dogs. Although these animals have been brought to bear very effectively because of their natural gifts in this area, a well-trained Tracker can also follow a Chase by his scent or other odors he has emitted.

Scent tracking is a difficult task for a human being. Our sense of smell is not as keen as an animal's, and a human's maximum capacity to smell has been greatly diminished due to lack of use in our modern civilization. Nonetheless, there is a whole array of familiar odors that can be recognized, identified, and used as clues throughout the course of a mission. The trick is to sensitize yourself to any and all of these, while quickly identifying the possible source. They include the following:

Smoke

Smoke is comprised of tiny particles of soot or ashes that are lighter than air and take on the appearance of a vapor or mist. Wood smoke is usually whitish, dusky, or gray in color and ranges in clarity from a thin transparent haze to a thick opaque cloud, depending on the amount of pitch or moisture contained within the wood. Smoke caused by petroleum products or chemicals takes on a black, thick appearance, and can contain

16 American Rescue Dog Association, *Search and Rescue Dogs, Training Methods* (New York: Macmillan General Reference, 1991): 22. Used by permission.

toxins that can disable or kill whoever inhales it. I'm sure we have all experienced the smell of cigar, cigarette, and pipe smoke, as well as that from a burning wood or charcoal fire in a fireplace or campsite. It goes without saying that the stronger the smell, the closer you may be to your Chase.

Cooking

Depending on the culture in which you were raised, cooking can leave either a pleasant or unpleasant aroma that can easily assist you in your search. Just as your mother's blueberry cobbler lured you to her kitchen, so can the smell of cooking in a wild and natural habitat lead you to your Chase.

Knowing ethnic differences between various cultures' food, flavors, and cooking styles can also provide critical clues to identifying your Chase. In order to learn these varied aromas, spend a little time in the international district of your closest large city. Learn to identify the differences between garlic and onions, kimchee, sauerkraut, Cajun jambalaya, sushi, and chitlins. Can you tell the difference between Italian and Mexican food? Chinese and Japanese spices? Cajun and Indian seasonings? German and Russian dishes? Korean and Vietnamese preferences? English and Australian styles? If you are in Korea, can you tell if the dinner you smell is Korean or Cambodian? You'd better be able to tell the difference. During the Vietnam War, many American soldiers were tracked down based on the food, deodorant, scented soaps, and shaving creams that they used. (One passive defensive action is to eat what the natives eat and bathe with what the natives use.)

Fuel

Smells emitted from cooking, lighting, or transportation fuels are quite different from smoke. In most cases, the emission is colorless and completely transparent unless improperly trimmed (as related to cooking or lighting fuels), choked, or sealed (as related to engines). This is another area in which experience is the key to proper identification and clue collection. You should know the difference in smell between fresh and burned leaded gasoline, unleaded gas, diesel fuel, and jet fuel; you should be able to differentiate between propane, kerosene, Sterno fuel, and natural gas; and you should know what burning candle wax, lamp oil, whale blubber, or various fish oils smell like when used for lighting purposes.

Body Odors

Even if the Chase does not slip up and expose himself through careless fires and cooking, he will almost never be able to control his own body odors. Even the cleanest individual will emit hygienic smells related to soaps, powders, shaving cream, deodorant, and colognes. Anyone who has ever participated in physical labor or a sporting event knows what a human being's sweat smells like, and it's not that much harder to differentiate between sweat emitted from a clean body and that emitted from an unclean, unkempt body. And while we are on the subject of sweat, animal sweat is also easy to differentiate. If your Chase is on a running horse, for instance, horse sweat is very easily identified and followed, if within a certain distance. Other transportation means have other smells. Can you tell the difference between a donkey, a camel, a goat, or even a llama—all of which can be used for transporting humans or their equipment? (I suppose I should also include elephants here, although I'm sure you would most likely see or hear one before you ever smelled it!)

Other body odors should also be considered. An unclean body that has been out in the woods for a week or more—even without strenuous activity—is bound to produce a rather potent smell. A woman's unattended menstrual period will also produce a strong and particular odor, as will human and animal urine and feces. The strongest (and most repulsive) of all natural odors to a human being is that of a dead and decomposing body of a person or animal.

Many factors will affect the scent of your Chase. One of these variables is wind direction in relation to your direction of movement. Is the wind blowing directly into your face, or is it coming from behind or from either side? If it is cold and windless, the odor will linger in a low area where the scent will be more constricted. If it is hot and humid, and perhaps windy, the scent is more likely to spread across a wider area with greater potency.

Any suspicious odor should put you immediately on the alert. In many cases, when you are close enough to smell your Chase, you are close enough for him to see you, and appropriate defensive actions should not be delayed.

TACTILE TRACKING

Tactile tracking refers to touch, one of the least used of our senses. Even in tracking, we depend mostly on our eyes, ears, and nose to locate our Chase, but tactile senses provide valuable clues that could furnish that elusive piece of information—regardless of whether you are in bright daylight or zero moonlight conditions.

The sense of touch encompasses a whole array of subcategories, just as our other senses do. Each of these must be examined to complete the full picture.

> *Moisture.* Compare the wetness or dryness of the sign you are examining against that of its surroundings.
>
> *Shape.* What is the outline of the object you are touching? Does it consist of a regular or irregular pattern? Is it flat, lumpy, square, or cylindrical?
>
> *Size.* This category includes the quantity of the objects (how many are there?) and the capacity or measurement of the object: its length, width, and height.
>
> *Temperature.* This again is measured against the sign's surroundings. Is it cooler or warmer than the ground, objects, or atmosphere that surrounds it? Is it fire-hot? Is it abnormally ice-cold?
>
> *Texture.* Is the sign or object smooth, or is it rough? What kind of texture does it have? Is the object rubbery? Glassy? Jagged? Sticky? Prickly?
>
> *Vibration.* Is the ground shaking? If you place your hand on the proverbial railroad track, can you feel it rumble? Is there a rhythm to the vibration?

The following could easily be a sensory tracking scenario.

The time is 0400 (4:00 a.m.). Illumination is zero (no moonlight). You come upon an abandoned campsite, and neither your flashlight nor night vision goggles are available or functioning. Better yet, let's say both items are working and available, but it is tactically unsound to use them for fear of compromise. As you approach the campsite, the slightest sound of crackling wood catches your attention, and a whiff of smoke draws you nearer to the center of what was once a campfire. When you are within six inches of the glowing cinders, you place your hand above the remnants of the wood and coals, letting it hover for a few seconds (temperature). Placing your hand at a safe, low level from the center of the dim, flickering embers, you begin a circular uncoiling movement to determine the diameter (size) of what seems to be a small campfire. You direct your hand to examine the border of the campfire—and it touches a metal (texture) cup (shape). A foot away from the dying campfire, you locate a large pair (size) of damp (moisture) boots (shape). Adjacent to the boots, suspended on a branch, is a wet (moisture) set of large (size) cotton (texture) briefs. While probing around some tall (size) elephant grass (texture), you feel three large (size) areas that have been pancaked; the flattened areas are cool to the touch (temperature), similar to the surrounding grasses. You then use your previously gathered information to deduce what this picture may be telling you.

• • •

Trained and honed, our senses are the most important factors in the pursuit of our Chase. If you use them properly, you, too, can turn your senses into scientific evidence-gathering machines.

In the next chapter we will discuss the fine points of what makes a sign a sign, and the factors which inhibit tracking ability.

THE PURSUIT: DAY ONE

As Rowe prepares the Cache Report, Samoa approaches Badilla and O'Connor. "The rest of the team will depart in thirty minutes, after we finish cross-loading equipment, pyro, and ammo. We will rendezvous with you at or near grid 334863, ten meters this side of the ridgeline. Go!"

Badilla and O'Connor quietly insert a fifteen-round magazine into their secondary weapon, a 9mm Beretta, and then lock and load a thirty-round magazine into their M-4 carbine rifles, adjusting the PVS7 night vision goggles on their heads. They start toward the area of the ridgeline on which they saw the infiltrators not two hours earlier, the frozen fog lifting even as the night grows ever darker with the approach of early morning nautical twilight, the darkest period before sunrise.

Badilla, the team's primary Tracker, and O'Connor, the coverman and secondary Tracker, are a two-person team unto themselves, having worked closely together for the past six years. The two know each other's roles, thoughts, and expected movements without words, their training taking over instinctively.

Badilla leads the way up the steep and rugged hillside toward the ridgeline, applying strict noise discipline and weaving around elephant grass, short evergreens, and deciduous trees. Five meters short of the crest, he lifts his non-shooting hand, fingers extending upward, giving O'Connor the hand and arm signal to halt. As he drops to one knee, he simultaneously pulls out his camouflage stick and rubs it against his face, reapplying what had worn off during the night. Without a word, O'Connor assumes security, as he scans the perimeter with his night vision goggles and sweeps his line of sight with his M-4, mounted with an infrared illuminator. Just as quickly as Badilla adopts the security posture, O'Connor applies his own camouflage.

For fifteen minutes, immediately after sunrise, this two-person team remains motionless, in tune with nature and alert for any sound, smell, or sight of the enemy before committing themselves over the crest of the ridge. Sensing nothing, they move slowly, methodically, the wind in their favor as they muffle the sounds of the residual, crisp leaves ridged with frost from the cold night. The fog lingers in the lowlands; the only sound they hear is the sound of their own heartbeats. With the index fingers of their shooting hands fully extended along the rifles' trigger guards, they are ready for whatever they may face on the opposite side of the ridge.

One meter before they reach the crest, they crouch as low as possible, taking cover behind two opposing trees. With one full harmonious sweep, they smoothly dominate their perimeter without a sound. Since they approached from the south, O'Connor dominates the position to their right, from east to north, while Badilla dominates the area to their left, from west to north. They once again remain still to look, listen, and smell. From far below in the valley they hear the faintest sounds of cowbells, and not far from their location the distinctive aroma of manure wafts in their direction from the ridgeline trail.

Badilla holds up his hand—5...4...3...2...1. Carefully, they step over the crest. Badilla scans the foreground, lifts his eyes to sweep the middle distance, and squints toward the far ground, looking for movement, smoke, glints of metal in the infant sunlight, anything that might give away their Chase's location. From his position and vantage point, O'Connor does the same. They see nothing out of the ordinary.

Without a word, they move eastward, encountering their first sign—a series of partial prints in a patch of trail that exposes the brown soil. They appear to be deep prints, as if from a boot or from an individual with a heavy weight, but they were indistinguishable. Continuing down the trail, they encounter their first obstacle, a Happy Mound, a traditional Korean burial site. There, on the far side of the Happy Mound, is an unmistakable pointer sign, a freshly broken branch indicating recent movement toward the east.

The voice of Gunnery Sergeant Kimble, Badilla's first tracking instructor who served three years in Vietnam as a Tracker/sniper, echoes in his head: "Never take a carrot in plain sight. It could be an Elmer's booby trap or ambush. Open your ears, nose, and eyes through and around your sign. What does your gut feeling say?"

His gut feeling tells him it is a valid sign.

The two men turn and make their way back to the rendezvous point, immediately south of the ridge in an area just large enough for the team to circle up in a tight meeting. Near- and far-side recognition signals are exchanged at Grid 334863. A successful linkup has been made.

Badilla and O'Connor disseminate to the team what they have discovered so far, concluding that the infiltrators most likely did continue eastward along the ridgeline trail past the point where the team observed them earlier in the morning. Jordan confirms from contact made with higher headquarters that there will be other teams shadowing and flanking their movements at approximately 500 meters to either side and to the team's rear, with biohazard materials experts standing by at a helo staging area thirty kilometers from their location. National Special Forces teams surreptitiously guard major dams and intersections. With all team members fully informed, they move out in the direction Badilla and O'Connor traveled minutes earlier.

Because of the steep terrain, the need for speed, and the low risk of encountering the enemy at this early stage of the pursuit, the team forms up in a file formation along the ridgeline. Badilla takes the lead Tracker position; O'Connor the coverman; Jordan, as team leader, positions himself in the center with Rowe, the radio operator, immediately to his rear, followed by Major Kim; Samoa assumes the responsibility for rear security.

As they approach the partial footprints, Badilla holds up the halt signal, and the team immediately takes a knee, rifles ready to the right, left, front, and rear of their location. Positioning himself behind the footprints, he flips open his compass and trains it in the direction of the Happy Mound, whispering the azimuth reading to O'Connor, who relays it to Jordan. Looking past the Happy Mound, he keys in on a rock formation twenty meters beyond and signals the team to move out.

Eyes sweeping to the front, right, left, up, down, near, and far, Badilla searches for any signs left by the infiltrators. Here, he stops to examine a clump of elephant grass, blades bent over and pointing eastward. There, he peers at a branch from a waist-high woody plant, its leaves bottom-side up with the dew disturbed. And farther beyond, he makes mental note of a spider's web torn from its moorings, its inhabitant hiding while waiting for the sun to signal a time for rebuilding. The pursuit leads them off the ridge and into the wooded valley.

Paralleling the Nonsan-Chon River, the team continues eastward. As they approach a split in the river, the trail starts to widen into a fording area crossing the river, and there are locals filling up water jars and buckets not fifty kilometers from their location.

Badilla signals a halt, and the team crouches in a defensive posture, straddling the trail. Bringing O'Connor with him, he moves forward toward the stream, trying to balance the need for caution against causing unnecessary alarm among those gathering water.

Many footprints crisscross through the area, including civilian footwear, boots, and hoofprints. Badilla smiles. The infiltrators have used smart strategy to ensure that their prints would be covered over by the many travelers crossing the stream. Then he stops and bends over, while O'Connor takes a knee and moves his gaze across a sweeping arc to their front and flanks, keeping a sharp eye on the civilians to his right.

There, in front of them at the water's edge, is a boot print, clearly imprinted into the muddy, pebbled dirt. There is no mistaking the tire-like tread, the medium wear, the military nature of the print before him. Badilla lays his rifle beside it, measuring it from heel to toe and side to side at the widest part and the heel. Pulling out his digital camera, he quickly snaps a picture of the imprint while O'Connor records the measurements, and then he looks at his map to note the grid coordinate of its location and the time of its discovery.

Badilla examines the print closely, looking for indicators of the passage of time since the print was made. The print is not filled with water, and the impression is sharp, indicating passage as recently as three hours earlier. The print is also deep, displacing the dirt on the edge—a clear indicator that the owner of this boot was carrying a heavy load. As this is a favorite place for local civilians to gather water, it would not be surprising for the infil-trators to use this for the same purpose. The possibilities swirl around his head.

After conducting a thorough search using the Tracker Observation Procedures, he and O'Connor return to the team and brief their leader.

"Military print, clear as day," Badilla reports, showing the digital photo to Jordan. "There appears to be possible remnants of other prints, but they were pretty well contaminated by the local traffic crossing the stream here. There also seemed to be evidence of someone being dragged for a short distance, but again, it was hard to tell underneath the more recent prints. From my observation, I would say the person who made the print was carrying a heavy load, most likely a large pack. If they used this as a water resupply site, they most likely have some kind of water purification."

Major Kim agrees with the assessment, confirming that the infiltrators will be well-supplied and well-trained veterans.

"How old is the print?" Jordan asks.

"Judging by the partially dried edges, I'd say pretty close to four hours," Badilla answers with confidence.

"We'll take a quick break, then keep going."

With the team at 50-percent alert, O'Connor makes quick work of his hasty meal and makes his way to the observation area, assuming the position of primary Tracker. He scouts the ground around the perimeter of the site, searching for the infiltrators' path upon their departure. After a short, circular pattern, he finds a trail of bent grass leading toward yet another log fallen over the river, this one beyond the intersection of the two streams. While he is shooting the azimuth and identifying his next checkpoint, the rest of the team comes up behind him and falls into their appropriate places in the formation.

They maneuver around a fallen log serving as a bridge over the Nonsan-Chon. They cross the log one at a time, hastily moving in and out of the open danger area on top of the fast-moving river. The trail leads them up the hillside to a new ridgeline. They move quickly from checkpoint to checkpoint, encouraged by the positive signs they had come across and not wanting to let their Chase gain any kind of a lead.

Throughout the afternoon, the team moves steadily along, stopping for unusual noises, signs, checkpoints, and note-taking. O'Connor finds and points out indicators that would be indistinguishable to the untrained eye—an overturned rock, bent branch, and scratched moss—and Badilla relays all relevant information to the team leader.

Late in the afternoon, O'Connor halts. The infiltrator team appears to have branched off the trail downhill to their right. The team closes ranks as they carefully pick their way through the vegetation toward a small area of clearing. On the edge of the glade, O'Connor and Badilla sharpen their gazes and their senses toward any sound, smell, or movement. Team members take staggered security positions with rifles ready as O'Connor moves forward, heart pounding as he enters the open area, hoping and praying for no peering eyes other than those of his team. No shots ring out, and he searches carefully around him for disturbed dirt, possible booby traps, or other signs left by the infiltrators.

Something catches his attention, and he signals for 360-degree security. When the team is in place, both he and Badilla move forward, the latter providing security for the pair's immediate surroundings. In front of him, O'Connor sees four areas of flattened grass, smaller than those of a sleep site, with circles of what appear to be burnt areas in front of three of them. With the pancaked areas as his starting point, he takes one careful step at a time in a circular pattern, attentively searching the ground as his path takes him in an ever-widening coil.

Around the flattened imprints, he sees cracker crumbs and kernels of small white rice. He reaches out his hand over one of the burnt areas, circling it palm down toward the ground until it touches the charred grass. It is cold. In fact, all the signs appear to be hours old. Satisfied with his and the team's safety at this point, he signals to the team to come forward.

"Looks like a meal halt. The flattened grass is smaller than we found earlier and in a circular pattern indicating all-around security. There are burnt areas on the ground outside the circle that look like they could have used some kind of heat source for cooking. And there are rice and cracker crumbs."

Major Kim examines the rice and crumbs. "This looks like rice that could have come from the northern region, but the crackers could be from anywhere, north or south."

Samoa offers his assessment. "These are professionals. Look at how they are sitting in a circle facing outward. And you can barely see any sign that they even ate anything. They are obviously careful in their security."

Jordan does not like what he is hearing. A team of professionals certainly puts his own team in greater danger. "You guys know what we are up against. Do your jobs but don't take any unnecessary chances." He looks up at the sun, now easing behind the mountain ridgelines. "Let's keep it going, but keep an eye out for a place to lay up for the night."

With Badilla at the point, the team continues eastward for an additional hour or so before Jordan calls a halt. With the sun setting and the rest of the team in a defensive posture, Jordan and Samoa move out to locate an appropriate sleep site off the main trail and away from curious eyes. Within thirty minutes, the site is found, the perimeter set up, and the schedule for security watch is discussed and understood.

Day One is over.

CHAPTER 4

What Happened to My Signs?

Neither in body nor in mind do we inhibit the world of those hunting races of the Paleolithic era. . . . Memories of their animal envoys still must sleep, somehow, within us; for they wake a little and stir when we venture into wilderness.

—JOSEPH CAMPBELL

In the last chapter, we touched on the subject of visual tracking, carried out by the most common of the human senses, sight. What we will discuss in this chapter are the substances that make up visual tracking—visible "signs." You will learn how to recognize the various signs and become familiar with those factors that influence the clarity of the traces or indicators left by your Chase.

Again, we will break these down into separate categories: ground, middle, and top signs. The imaginary line that differentiates a ground from a middle sign can be found at ankle level. A ground sign leaves an imprint or other disturbance on the earth, while a middle sign affects that area above the ground that starts at ankle level and extends to the height and width of the Chase (including his equipment) and beyond. A top sign, then, is anything above eye level and could include anything in or on trees, caves, or cliffs (like snipers. Yikes!).

GROUND SIGNS

The potential list of all the possible ground signs is obviously too extensive to cover completely in a limited volume such as this. The following, however, are examples of the types of signs you can expect to encounter.

Footprints

The most common example of what one might consider a ground sign is a footprint, whether left by a bare foot, shoe, sneaker, boot, or other kind of footwear. It could either be a clearly defined print in mud or clay, or it could be mud dropped from a boot onto a hard surface in a formless residue. The print could also be a vague mark or scratch on the surface that follows along the predetermined stride of the Chase (more on that later) and can be reasonably assumed to be a footprint. What is included here would be bruised or "bleeding" roots, crushed ground vegetation or leaves, or other disturbances of grass, vegetation, rocks, or twigs.

Other Prints

Another example is a different kind of print, left by something other than a foot. This could include an imprint of one's buttocks (see figure 4.1), other parts of the human body, or equipment placed on the ground in

Figure 4.1 Person at rest—sitting.

irregular patterns. Usually this would indicate a place of rest, sleep, or meal-taking.

Disturbances

Yet another kind of ground sign is a disruption of nature. This includes a disturbance of insect life, such as a highly active beehive or scattered anthill (see figures 4.2A and B). Another example would be agitation of

Figure 4.2A Anthill—undisturbed.

Figure 4.2B Anthill—disturbed.

Figure 4.3 Water disturbance.

water, such as mud swirling in an otherwise clear puddle, pond, or slow-moving stream (see figure 4.3); splatter marks (see figures 4.4A and B); or ripples in small bodies of water for which there is no other apparent cause (such as wind). It also includes, as mentioned earlier, other disturbances of ground vegetation, rocks, or twigs.

Of course, some of the most noticeable ground signs are those left by a careless Chase. These are signs that are obviously not of a natural origin, such as discarded cigarette butts, trash, wire, or food particles.

Figure 4.4A Splatter marks.

Figure 4.4B Splatter marks/water transfer.

MIDDLE SIGNS

Looking above ankle level, one can often find clear signs left by the Chase. As described above, middle signs can also include disturbances of insect life but at a higher level, such as overactive beehives or torn spiderwebs (see figure 4.5). Vegetation may be discolored or left in an unnatural position—most likely in the direction of movement. There may be cuts or scratches on trees, or you may encounter broken twigs and leaves. Bent tree limbs or leaves will also identify the direction of travel (see figure 4.6).

If you are at a good vantage point and see the swaying of trees or movement of grass or bushes, you can reach two different conclusions. One, the wind is causing the movement; or two, if the wind is not blowing or if it is blowing in a direction at odds with what you are seeing, you can

Figure 4.5 Torn spiderweb.

Figure 4.6 Leaf identifying direction of travel.

Figure 4.7 Ascend incline.

definitely say that a person or animal is moving the trees or bushes. Many times, a person will use trees or branches to help him ascend or descend a steep area (see figure 4.7), making such movement obvious to an astute observer.

Wind Speed

For many reasons, a good Tracker should be able to estimate wind speeds. A gunnery sergeant in the Marine Corps taught me to look at my surroundings to estimate the speed of the wind (see figure 4.8). Now, all of our teams must commit these facts to memory. By combining the senses of sight and touch (feeling), nature can tell you much of what is happening.

In arid, hot desert land, wind estimate is based on the wind's actual effect on the "mirage," the glassy or water-like appearance of the heated terrain, as seen through the naked eye or binoculars (see figure 4.9).

MPH	Effects
0–1	Smoke rising straight up (flag lying flat against the pole)
1–3	Leaves and smoke in motion
4–7	Wind sensation felt on face; leaves fluttering
8–12	bility to view undersides of leaves remaining on trees; grounded leaves (deadfall) and/or loose paper lifted
13–18	Small branches swaying; fallen leaves (deadfall) and trashed paper blown and swept along the ground
19–24	Large branches and small trees swaying; dust clouds rising

Figure 4.8 Estimate of wind speed based on the wind's impact.

MPH	Appearance	Effects
0–1	‖	Mirage or smoke rising straight up (flag lying flat against the pole)
3–5		Mirage or smoke in motion to the left
3–5		Mirage or smoke in motion to the right
5–8		Mirage, air vapors are close together and horizontal; wind sensation on skin; moving ground debris
8–12		Mirage, air vapors are widely spaced out and horizontal; loose debris being lifted; small amounts of shifting sand

Figure 4.9 Estimate of wind speed based in hot, arid desert.

TOP SIGNS

Perhaps one of the greatest mistakes many novice Trackers make is failing to look up. The most dangerous objects are often just above eye level, in trees, cliffs, or caves. That is where you will find some of the world's deadliest snakes, predatory cats, and dangerous human beings—with spotting scope and sniper rifle aimed in your direction. From those hiding or escaping in a hurry, this is the area that may yield the most visible signs, such as scrapes on branches or rocks, or gouges in hillside soils. There, you may find cave or tree dwellers of the harmless variety (bats, squirrels, monkeys), but pay close attention if these dwellers are agitated or disturbed. While looking up is especially recommended for those seeking life's most profound answers, it is also beneficial—and potentially life-saving—for the ordinary Tracker in the field.

Whatever the category, some signs are easier to locate than others. Certain places are more likely than others to either cause or expose signs. These are the points at which we need to be the most alert, especially if we have temporarily lost the trail. Areas where signs can be easily found include steep hillsides, thick undergrowth or tall grass, muddy or sandy patches, embankments or rivers or streams, edges of clearings, firebreaks, or any other location where obstacles need to be crossed or the Chase's route is canalized. In these places, the Chase cannot help but leave distinguishing marks, tracks, or other evidence of being there.

MEASURING

Before getting into the nuts and bolts of measuring prints and strides, one must understand the mechanics behind the human step. When walking, a human being tends to contact the ground with a heel first, rolling then to the ball of the foot, then to the toes. If there are no physical problems, the weight is evenly distributed along the entire foot. If the Chase is disabled in some fashion or injured, you may find that he drags a foot, distributes more weight on his right or left leg, or walks on the side of his foot.

As with a fingerprint, no two shoe prints are alike. Even without disability or injury, some people just have a tendency to place more emphasis on the balls of their feet, while others walk "pigeon-toed," slant their toes outward, or place more weight on the sides of their feet. An individual's size, weight, and posture also have a lot to do with weight distribution. Likewise, attitude plays a large part. One print may be made by a "cool cat" or "dude" dipping his head while walking and thinking, "Yeah, man. I'm bad. I'm cool!" Another may be made by a physically fit, mentally disciplined individual smoothly striding down the path. Yet another may be left by an older, more tentative individual shuffling along the road. That is why I have always said that every sign fits into a specific category; every sign is distinctly characteristic and leaves me with a direct reflection and/ or impression of my Chase.

Once you have been tracking someone for an hour or so, you should be able to draw some conclusion about the Chase's stride, size of print, and pattern of shoe (see figure 4.10). Even in the midst of other human tracks, such as in a contaminated tracked area (see figure 4.11), you should still be able to distinguish your Chase's print from any other human print.

In order to do this conclusively, however, you will need to scientifically analyze your Chase's print and stride.

Figure 4.10 Distinguishing print.

Figure 4.11 Contaminated prints.

Of course, the first thing you need to do is to sketch or photograph (with a digital or Polaroid camera) the actual pattern of the Chase's shoe or boot. Keep in mind that prints can be concave due to very soft soil—like loose, dry sand—or they can be pancaked due to patternless undersoles without heels. On the other hand, prints can also be very well defined with an abundance of sole patterns, leaving a regularity of clear characteristics that may even include the brand name of the shoe. This, naturally, depends on the composition and density of the soil. The maintenance and sustainability of a pattern are also totally at the mercy of animal signs, other human signs, terrain, climatic conditions, and time.

Once you have established the distinct characteristics of your Chase's footprint, the next logical step is to determine his stride. In 1981, a Malaysian major—who headhunted many insurgent guerrillas in his native country—taught me to use my M16A1 rifle to measure the size of a print and the stride of my Chase. Those on a search and rescue mission can just as easily use a sturdy walking stick or ski pole at least four feet in length.

Stride is defined as the distance between the left and right footprint of an individual walking normally. Measure the stride heel to heel, placing the butt of your newly converted measuring instrument (weapon, stick, or pole) on the rearward edge (heel) of the forward shoe print and working your way back to the most rearward edge (heel) of the rear print. Mark your weapon or stick. This measurement will gauge your Chase's stride (see figures 4.12A and B). This may seem like we are measuring the print backward, from front to rear rather than from rear to front, which is the direction of travel. But remember, a tracker team must constantly look from the farthest point to the nearest point in order to maintain security. Likewise, these measurements must follow the same guidelines.

You can also use the weapon or stick to locate a second print if only one is visible. By using it as a pivot point from the known impression, you can estimate an average stride and sweep it from side to side to locate the second one.

The length of any one shoe print is the distance between the rearward edge or heel to the most forward edge or toe of the same print. I would advise using the same stick or weapon that was used to mark the Chase's stride. After marking the stride at the heel of the forward print, keep the

Figure 4.12A Stride and Saddle measurement—tape (see appendix A "Human Profile Card").

Figure 4.12B Stride and Saddle measurement—weapon (see appendix A "Human Profile Card").

Figure 4.13A Print measurement—tape.

Figure 4.13B Print measurement—weapon.

weapon or stick in the same position and make an additional mark at the print's toe, measuring its length (see figures 4.13A and B).

The width of the shoe print should be measured in two areas: the widest portion, or ball of the foot (see figures 4.14A and B), and then at the

Figure 4.14A Ball of foot measurement—tape.

Figure 4.14B Ball of foot measurement—weapon.

heel (see figures 4.15A and B). These marks should also be made on your weapon or stick, continuing from the previous mark on the shoe length.

To mark your weapon, stick, or pole effectively, you can choose from a number of markers, based on what you have available. Some people use a

Figure 4.15A Heel measurement—tape.

Figure 4.15B Heel measurement—weapon.

knife to mark their measuring stick; others may prefer a permanent bright marker, grease pencil, or rubber band. Just keep in mind that whatever you use must be able to withstand the normal usage of your "measuring instrument." A rubber band will most likely melt on the barrel of a rifle that has been fired repeatedly; if a rubber band is all you have available, consider turning the weapon around when measuring, starting with the tip of the weapon and working your way toward the butt. The stride will most likely be longer than the rifle barrel, and the first rubber band will be located closer to the trigger assembly or handle. On the other hand, if you are high in the mountains on skis and need to use a ski pole to measure, a magic marker may not write on a frozen pole. A rubber band may freeze, move, or break during the pole's normal usage. If you are very familiar with your instrument of measure and have an excellent memory, making a mental note may be just as effective.

FACTORS AFFECTING SIGNS

There are four factors that can unfavorably affect your tracking ability. They are the signs left by those other than your Chase (for instance, by other humans or animals), terrain over which the Chase is moving, climatic weather conditions, and time since the sign was left. All of these factors are closely tied together and can either inhibit or aid in your search.

Other Humans and Animals

Unless you are in a totally uninhabited area of the world, other people will most likely affect your search. Hikers, hunters, forest rangers, farmers, or area residents may contaminate signs left by your Chase. They may leave their own footprints or unnatural disturbances, which may be indistinguishable from the Chase's.

On the other hand, while incidental prints and signs may affect those of your Chase, other people in the area can also aid in your search. Talk to the people you run across. They may have seen or heard something that could put you back on the trail or lead you much closer to your Chase.

Animals can be used in much the same way. Now obviously, an animal cannot speak. But they can give us other indicators that can bring us closer to our Chase. As I pointed out in chapter 3, many animals and insects will warn us of other humans or the presence of danger. Birds will flock away in a panic when approached by a person or predatory animal; insects will become silent when someone tramples their area; and monkeys will sound off when humans or other animals invade their territory. Again, to become a successful Tracker, it is necessary to familiarize yourself with the indigenous wildlife in your area.

Yet, just as humans can contaminate or otherwise affect a trail of signs, animals can, too—and they do it much more often. There are many excellent reference books that cover the specifics of animal tracks, so I will not go into that subject here. But keep in mind that all animals, whether they fly, swim, slither, walk, or hop, have their own distinct imprints.

The Chase, in order to deceive a Tracker, may replicate an animal's imprint, but it will never be exact. A skilled Tracker can easily tell the difference.

Terrain

In order to effectively track people through wilderness areas, the Tracker must become intimately familiar with the terrain and foliage of the tracking area. And, as I mentioned in previous sections, the terrain can assist or detract from your efforts, depending on your knowledge of various land features and your tracking experience. Most likely, you will be confronted with one or more of the following terrain types: grassland, rain forest, wetlands, rocky ground, and sand.

Grassland. The condition of the grasses over which the Chase is traveling will determine the ease with which you can find him. If the grass is green, resilient, and short, the grass will spring back up to its normal state quite rapidly once trampled on. If the grass is wet from the previous night's dewfall, any travel across this grass will be quickly and easily noticed; you will see a difference in the grass color where the dew has been rubbed off (see figure 4.16). In some instances, you may find dirt clumps or sand in places where the Chase stepped after picking up loose or moist dirt.

If the grassy area is sparse and the surrounding soil is moist, you should find a clear imprint in the dirt as well as soil residue farther down on the grass where it has been transferred (see figures 4.17A and B).

Tall grass, higher than a foot and a half, will greatly simplify the location of your Chase. Tall grass, when trodden, will not spring back to its original position. On the other hand, it interlaces and points in the

Figure 4.16 Prints in morning dew/frost.

direction of travel (see figure 4.18). If the grass is green, the undergrowth is lighter, showing a discoloration; if the grass is dry, the result will be choppy, broken, and/or crushed stems (see figures 4.19A and B). You may also notice more prints around the dry grass.

Figure 4.17A Prints in sparse vegetation.

Figure 4.17B Prints in sparse vegetation, closer view.

Figure 4.18 Tall grass pointers.

Rain Forest. The foliage and terrain features of a rain forest provide ample opportunity to effectively track your Chase. In triple-canopy jungles or heavily wooded evergreen forests, there is less undergrowth but better visibility of tracks or prints. Secondary jungles, on the other hand, produce a heavy undergrowth. Not only is there a great deal of tall, full-leafed trees and dense underbrush, including thick blankets of plants, bushes, briars, vines, and moss, but there is also an abundance of geological features, such as rocks, streams, mud, and sand. You will also encounter much deadfall.

*Figure 4.19A Print and
tall grass pointers.*

*Figure 4.19B Tall grass
pointers.*

Figure 4.20 Disturbed deadfall pointer and print.

Deadfall includes all manner of dead plant life, and each species presents its own unique means of identifying an individual who has crossed its path.

A tree fallen across a pathway provides an excellent opportunity to discover signs. Most likely, you will find prints or disturbances on either side of the tree (see figure 4.20). If it is a large tree, you can expect to find a print or scuff mark on the bark or a disturbance on the moss growing on the tree trunk. Similarly, a tree fallen over a river or stream may reveal not only splatter marks and prints, but may also reveal the Chase's direction of travel as he crossed over the water obstacle (see figure 4.21).

Leaves and branches provide other excellent opportunities for signs. Dry twigs and leaves become very frail and will crack and break under the pressure of any individual, even that of an infant. An aged leaf lying on the ground will still show signs of wetness from dew, although it has not rained. If disturbed, the leaf may tear, disintegrate, or simply discolor; it may just show a slick wetness in the area of disturbance, which can be easily distinguished from the translucent beads of dew.

Figure 4.21 Prints on log crossing.

Live leaves on bushes and trees, when turned over, bent, or twisted, will display a lighter shade of color as the underside is turned sideways or upward. Some turned leaves look almost white when compared with the same type of undisturbed leaves. These leaves are white flags to the astute Tracker (see figure 4.22).

Let's not forget the tiniest inhabitants of the rain forest. Insects can be invaluable to the observant Tracker, especially the "creepy crawlers"—ants and spiders. Disturbed ant trails or hills and broken spiderwebs (refer back to figures 4.2 and 4.5) are indicators that someone or some animal has passed along this same passage. In a similar way, dead grasshoppers, bees, or other types of insects may also provide pertinent clues.

Figure 4.22 Underside of leaves exposed.

Wetlands. As the word indicates, wetlands are more than just swampy or marshy areas. They include any moving or stationary body of water, such as rivers and streams, lakes and ponds, as well as tidal flats, mangroves, swamps, and bayous. While presenting obvious challenges to the novice Tracker, many characteristics of the various wetlands actually assist the Tracker.

Scores of movies have relied upon the clichéd and ever-present river or stream to help the film's hero shake his pursuers. It would appear that once a person enters the water, he has successfully shaken the best of Trackers. While this may be an effective anti-tracking technique, it is not a method that makes it impossible to find or follow a Chase's track or signs (see figure 4.23). In fact, there are many areas—not only around rivers or streams but also around lakes, ponds, and other wetlands—that are prime locations for signs (see figures 4.24A and B).

Look carefully around the edges of banks, where the soil is constantly moist and the rocks are often loose. Here, footprints are most likely to stand out clearly. Take a closer look at the shallow water just inside the water's edge. Is there an obvious print or disturbance in the silt, pebbles, or sand? Is the mud stirred up? If there are rocks lining the edge of the water,

Figure 4.23 Prints in water.

Figure 4.24A Prints near water.

Figure 4.24B Prints near body of water (sand).

are there scrapes or scuff marks, which might indicate a sudden jump off or exertion to climb up? (See figure 4.25.) Are there dried water marks or droplets splashed on the rocks near the water or in crevices farther from the water? (See figure 4.26.)

Marshy ground presents a more difficult challenge. Because such "ground" is low, wet, and soft, distinct patterns of a print will not be so evident. Nonetheless, the stride will still be clear and measurable, and the print-like impression or concave filled with water can easily be noted. A wise Chase who does not want to be found likely knows this, too. He may then choose to leap near the base of trees, where the ground is "terra firma." An equally wise Tracker will also examine the base of trees for scratches or transferred mud.

Rocky Ground. While pioneers and modern-day moviegoers marvel at the ease with which Native Americans can track people over rocks, the feat is

Figure 4.25 Scuff marks on moss.

Figure 4.26 Water on rocks.

Figure 4.27 Print near water.

not as difficult as one would think. In fact, it is somewhat easy to track people over this type of terrain.

When referring to rocky ground, most people first think of mountainous terrain. In fact, much of our earth consists of this type of terrain. There exist three classes of rock: igneous, metamorphic, and sedimentary. Anyone who has ever studied rocks in their various forms will notice distinct differences, depending upon the climate and terrain in which they have been found. Some rocks are extremely hard and relatively immovable; others are very brittle and break off at the slightest disturbance.

Stones or rocks, when moved either deliberately or inadvertently, leave definite impressions in the surrounding soil. There is also a distinct contrast in color. If the ground is moist, the undersides of the stones and rocks will be drier and therefore lighter. In contrast, if the ground is dry, the undersides will remain damp and therefore darker.

Unless the Chase is wearing moccasins or soft-soled tennis shoes, he will likely leave scratches when moving across large rocks. If stones are crumbly, they will chip or crumble even more when trodden upon. Stones and pebbles sitting on soft soil are easily pushed down, leaving an indentation while simultaneously squeezing out the displaced soil (see figure 4.27).

Sand. While rocky ground seems to be one of the most difficult terrain features over which to track a Chase, sandy soil, at first look, seems to be

70

the easiest, with no foliage or water to hide the prints. There are, however, many threats to the integrity of a sand print, and these include the wind, rain, and—along the ocean shoreline—flood currents. Sand is a very fragile substance, and these elements show it no mercy; any signs left by your Chase will be rapidly eroded and defaced. If the sandy surface is hot, dry, and soft, you will see a concave impression where a foot has stepped, and you can measure the stride and relative size of the print. Yet, even the most detailed possible imprint is left to the mercy of climatic factors that will rapidly obliterate the sign.

Climatic Weather Conditions

Direct sunlight or moonlight can change the characteristics of a sign to the point that it appears to revert back to its natural state. Where there are no shadows present or contrasts evident, it is extremely difficult for a Tracker to make out a definitive shape of an imprint. Similarly, direct sunlight causes the rapid evaporation of a pure water print on a rock or other hard surface. In snow, also, a shallow print will quickly dissolve and turn to slush, leaving little or no trace.

Under other conditions, sun and moonlight can aid you. Let's just say that the snow-turned-slush our Chase was walking across earlier started to freeze from a drop in temperature. At this point, the Chase has left barely concave prints. As evening approaches, a full moon rises and an inch of snow covers his crossing. The shadows cast by the moon into the concave prints will clearly show his trail.

For this same reason, early morning, late evening, moonrise, and moonset are the best times to clearly identify a print. When the light source is directly on top of the observed object, such as a footprint, it is extremely hard to see due to the shortened shadow. On the other hand, light cast from the side or at an angle to the print (by the sun, moon, or artificial source) will cast a longer and more definitive shadow.

Trackers can take steps to aid in shadow-casting, even in direct moonlight or sunlight. During the day, Trackers can shade a suspected print with their body or other means, using a mirror or similar object to catch the sunlight and direct it at an angle toward the examined area—creating a cast shadow. Similarly, at night, Trackers can use flashlights, vehicle lights (although not in a tactical situation), or night vision goggles with infrared optics to define an otherwise invisible imprint. A New Zealand Tracker taught me to utilize a variety of colored lights for this, since any light other than natural light is compromising. Blue light is best for snowy areas; yellow light is best for arid sandy areas and/or dry grass; red is best in forested or dark areas.

Snow creates a unique set of both challenges and opportunities. One of the first things I learned about snow was never to eat yellow or brown snow. While this may seem a no-brainer, yellow or brown discolorations can also indicate that the snow has been contaminated by human or animal urine or defecation. Depending upon the condition of the sign, one can make assumptions about the condition of the Chase, as I indicated in chapter 3 (what color is the urine, and what is the appearance of the feces).

Wet snow, with temperatures averaging thirty-two degrees Fahrenheit, will allow easy tracking of your Chase because the snow naturally compresses and holds that impression indefinitely with steady conditions. Take that same snow with shifting temperatures and added snowfall, and your Chase's tracks could be nearly obscured.

Dry, powdery snow, on the other hand, is as bad or worse than fine, drifting sand. It does not have the cohesiveness of wet snow and will not allow a discernible print to form, especially during shifting winds.

Strong winds, heavy rains, and snowfall are the three climatic conditions that will cause you the most severe problems while tracking your Chase. Wind and heavy rains are the *most* destructive enemies of the Tracker, causing direct and irreparable damage to signs you are trying hard to follow.

Strong winds will hasten the return of disturbed vegetation back to its natural state. They stir up dead leaves, sway trees and bushes, and cause ripples along bodies of water, covering up similar signs caused by the Chase. They conceal ground signs imprinted in sand, snow, water, or dry soil. They can also produce sandstorms, sand dunes, and large snowdrifts, while shifting sand and snow can threaten Tracker or Chase with severe vertigo. Anyone who has ever been in the soft desert plains or mountain whiteout conditions can easily identify with this effect.

They can also produce collateral noise from swaying trees, bristling bushes, and swirling leaves and branches, which cover up noise made by the Chase. But winds can also work in the Tracker's favor. If the Chase is upwind and the Tracker downwind, it can carry the Chase's noise toward the Tracker while simultaneously cloaking the noise the Tracker may be making. It can also carry smells in the direction of the Tracker, giving him a strong indication of the Chase's actions and location, allowing him to track with ease.

Rain is one element that will wash out nearly any ground sign not sheltered in some manner. In Central America, I have seen torrential rains fall so hard that it takes only minutes to create impromptu streams four feet wide and three feet deep where before there were none. The force of these streams will carry away anything in their path, including people, animals, homes, and large trees, and will most definitely wash out any previously imprinted signs.

But here, too, even rain can assist the Tracker. After a heavy or pro-longed rain, the ground in low-lying areas—such as draws or flat plains—will become soft and moist. Any individual who walks on this very soft, moist ground will leave clearly defined prints, sometimes as deep as two or three inches. If water has collected in the print, leaving a puddle that has not yet drained, one can fairly certainly conclude that the print may have been left within approximately two hours. (See chapter 5 on determining the age of signs.)

Of course, all of the above elements will unfavorably affect the signs left by the Chase, but the degree to which they will affect them will be based on the intensity and force levied on the signs. If impacted only by light rainfalls, mild winds, and subtle amounts of sunlight, or if they were sheltered by a canopy of some kind, these signs could still be recognizable for up to thirty or forty hours.

Time

One of the hardest tasks Trackers have before them is determining the time lapse between when the sign was made and when it was found. Because of the inherent difficulty and complexity, I have devoted the next chapter to exploring this single factor.

THE PURSUIT: DAY TWO

Stand to: The members of Detachment 266, at 50-percent security, quietly pack up their gear in the light morning drizzle, as the darkness of the night softens to a misty grayness. The weather has changed overnight, the increasing clouds giving way to a soft, steady sprinkle.

Badilla and O'Connor give each other knowing looks of satisfaction and eagerness, for they know, as does the rest of the team, that such a rain will only help in their pursuit.

As they hoist their fifty-pound rucks onto their shoulders, Badilla takes the lead position, having already scouted and reestablished the Chase's path from the previous night. He leads the team back onto the main trail and uphill, until they are once again just short of a ridgeline. He signals the halt and points to himself, O'Connor, and the ridgeline.

While the team automatically assumes a security posture, the two Trackers move cautiously toward the crest, pausing, examining, listening, and looking for any signs of hostile intent. Once on the trail, the two start east, Badilla alternately sweeping the landscape around him and examining the trail, vegetation, and terrain nearby.

After proceeding for about ten meters, Badilla halts. As O'Connor takes a knee beside him, rifle ready, Badilla whispers to him, "I see no signs of the Chase this way. Let's try west for twenty meters and see what that gets us. We may need to do an initial search procedure or a probing search to pick up the trail."

Badilla and O'Connor reverse directions, the medic much more watchful behind them since the remainder of their team is protecting their front. As they pass the place where the team is waiting, Badilla signals their intention to Jordan, who nods an acknowledgment.

The Tracker and coverman proceed west from the team, Badilla's eyes darting left to right, far to near. He sees many footprints on the well-worn, damp trail, but none that indicate a recent passage—at least since the rain began falling. Many imprints seem to be deeper than others, and Badilla makes a mental note of the possible heavy load that may have caused the deeper print, the gouges in the otherwise smooth grass. He notices leaves torn from brush and trees at chest-high levels, in areas that an unburdened person can easily pass without disturbing the vegetation. Satisfied, he signals the rest of the team to join up.

They continue at a faster speed along the crest trail, the signs found ensuring them that no infiltrators have passed by that way since the rain began hours before, in the early morning darkness. As they travel along the trail, they begin to see local residents with various farm animals. In a hasty yet careful hurry, the team disappears into the wood line, allowing the residents to pass without notice. Badilla, for his part, is beginning to strain to see foot-related signs, as they are quickly hidden beneath the many farmers' boot prints and their animals' hoofprints.

After moving rapidly for nearly one kilometer, Badilla suddenly slows where the trail branches downhill to his left. The deeper impressions he has been following seem to take a left at this point. Foliage at the edge of this trail contains broken branch pointers and overturned leaves. He also notices a deep scar and overturned rocks, which may indicate a person slipping on the steep terrain.

Badilla sends O'Connor and Rowe, as temporary Tracker and coverman, 10 meters farther down the original crestline path to ensure that there is no longer any evidence of deep impressions or pointer signs that may indicate people carrying heavy equipment. In minutes, they both return with a negative report.

Convinced that the infiltrators have taken a turn down the hill, Badilla also turns left and starts the descent while the team follows, trying with some difficulty to keep from slipping on the now damp trail grass. Within a few hundred meters, the trail begins to level out as it approaches the Yong Chiang Stream, and the foliage begins to thicken as the team nears the water's edge. Badilla signals a halt.

The team once again assumes the security position, as Badilla and O'Connor move forward. In front of them are distinct areas of flattening, about the size of a person lying down. Carefully picking their way around these areas, Badilla closely examines the ground. He picks up what appears to be small rubber shavings, which are black and white and tubular in shape. Upon further examination of the site, he finds the clear and unmistakable print of a rifle butt—one that could not be an M-4 or M-16 of the US and ROK forces.

After shooting a digital picture and making notes of his observation, he signals for the rest of the team, which meets him just outside the observation area.

"It appears that we have a sleeping site," Badilla explains to Jordan and the team. "Over there to the left are three flattened areas. According to the pattern, they appear to have been used as sleeping locations. Right off to the side over here," he shows them the sign on the ground, "is an imprint of a rifle stock."

Major Kim takes a closer look. "This is AK-47. For certain."

Jordan nods. "They aren't feeling very secure if they are leaving one person to stand guard while they sleep."

Badilla shows the leader the rubber shavings. "This appears to be rubber coating stripped off of some kind of copper wire—I can only guess at this point whether it was used for communications or an explosive device. Note the clean cuts on the pieces of rubber."

Rowe picked up a tiny rubber shaving. "There is no metallic residue on this, so I don't think it was cut or stripped with a pocketknife. They must have cut this with professional wire-cutting pliers."

Jordan sums up the findings. "We'll have to assume either communications equipment or an improvised explosive device. It appears that they definitely have AK-47s at their disposal."

Badilla makes additional notes in his small notebook.

"Anything else we need to know?" asks Jordan.

"Yeah," Badilla answers. "We are catching up to them. That rifle imprint is no more than three hours old."

Jordan turns to the team sergeant. "Samoa?"

"It appears to me from what we've seen so far that we have four, maybe five people who are good at hiding their tracks and are well equipped, with possible communications or explosives devices. The fact that we saw four flattened sitting areas and three burn spots right next to them may mean that the fourth is a captive, since he didn't get to cook. That may explain the dragging marks in the mud that Badilla saw yesterday."

O'Connor adds his observations. "Maybe that's why we're catching up. Even though we're following trained professionals, a civilian captive would certainly slow them down quite a bit."

Jordan turns to his radio operator. "Rowe, let me have that radio. I'd better call this in, just in case."

Higher headquarters orders them to keep up the pursuit and close the gap, while remaining out of sight and sound from the enemy. Intelligence reports indicate that local civilians have indeed seen what appear to be armed Adidas-clad Korean soldiers with a bound individual who looks to be a farmworker of some kind. The team is to use extreme caution to not harm the noncombatant.

Updated orders in hand, the team moves out, crossing the stream and following the much clearer trail to the south. The soft rain has continued to fall.

O'Connor is now in the primary tracking position, leading the team back uphill and along terrain that falls sharply toward a stream at least 800 feet below them. He is not the only one who warily eyes the drop-off on his left. A short distance along the ridge, they come across a knoll with a Happy Mound on it. O'Connor circles it and again picks up the familiar trail, now descending toward the Bagdoe Chon River.

Along the way, he notices a slight increase in the amount of middle signs at waist and shoulder height, most likely due to the increased thickness of the vegetation. "Makes my job much easier," he thinks as he comes across another pointer.

As the team gets close to the river, the men see a large tree lying across it, the deadfall serving as a makeshift bridge over the fast-moving water. O'Connor and Badilla carefully approach the tree, the former examining the bark while the latter scans their surroundings. There appear to be recent cuts and scuff marks, obviously not made by the native footwear of the locals and most likely caused by military-style boots. O'Connor can't easily tell the age of the marks, the constant drizzle masking the age-defining evidence. He sniffs at the overturned moss, the fresh dirt smell indicating it was recently shifted—no more than two hours earlier.

Once across, O'Connor and Badilla wait for the others to join them before they continue their tracking. When O'Connor rounds a tree on his right, he calls a halt and drops to a knee. In front of him is a small glade in which there is evidence of flattening.

He immediately embarks on the grid method Tracker Observation Procedures to search the entire area. What he finds is four definite areas of flattening in an all-around defensive posture, with a possible fifth area of flattening near what could be their perimeter. He documents the signs and returns to the team to fill them in.

"The compression of the flattened sites indicates that we may have gained even more ground. My estimate is maybe two hours old."

Badilla offers his estimate. "They aren't even looking behind them for anyone, or the signs would be much more pronounced. With a civilian slowing them down and no reason to hurry, we can easily gain another thirty minutes to an hour on them tonight."

Samoa gives his opinion to the waiting commander. "The weather report indicates a full moon and plenty of cloud breaks, so I say let's keep pushing on until we can't see anymore and then a little farther with night vision goggles. If we keep gaining on them like this, we can have those suckers sometime tomorrow, before they reach any inhabited areas."

Jordan nods his agreement and allows the team to catch a quick meal break while he calls in another report and informs headquarters of their intent. That requirement out of the way, the team moves out again, following Badilla as the Tracker.

Badilla's abilities are stretched to the limit as he feels the mounting pressure of locating definitive signs, watching for booby traps, and keeping the team moving at a rapid pace. His extensive training and experience extend his ability to do this effectively over any other member of the team.

He leads them along the edge of the river until the trail once again ascends onto the ridgeline. With night falling rapidly, the men pause only to don their night vision goggles. They steadily push themselves until the clouds cover the light from the full moon. They now stop for the night—or what few hours remain of it—atop a small hill. In the morning, they will be able to see far and wide in all directions, hopeful of a small glimpse of the Chase.

As the first man prepares to stand guard, Day Two comes to a close.

CHAPTER 5

How Long Has It Been Since We Last Met?

Time present and time past are both perhaps present in
time future. And time future is contained in time past.
—T. S. ELIOT

In chapter 3, we learned how to use all of our senses to fully "see" what was already before us. Chapter 4 taught us how to differentiate between different types of visual signs and how to tell the difference between a natural occurrence and an actual sign left by our Chase. Identifying a sign is great, but identification alone cannot tell us much about the Chase's current location. Can you judge the sign's age? Can you tell how long it's been there and how long ago the Chase passed this way?

One of the most difficult things a Tracker must learn is to determine how much time has elapsed since a sign was made. This is perhaps the most mysterious element to those who are unschooled in tracking, the one element that elicits the greatest awe from the non-Tracker. But, like the sights, sounds, and smells spoken of earlier, one must simply learn to *read* and *interpret* what is already there.

Even a novice Tracker should be able to make a reasonable assumption about the age of any sign. And as with anything else, practice will give you the edge you need when it really counts.

HUMAN AND ANIMAL EXCREMENT

In chapter 3, we discussed various odors, including that of human and animal urine and feces. Let's take that a step further and use that excrement to help us determine the passage of time. Chapter 1 included an excerpt in which a Native American Tracker examined horse droppings and determined not only the specific grasslands where the animal had grazed but also how much time had gone by since the droppings had been left. While not an exact science, determining time passage can be accomplished with a few clues.

Take a close look at the excrement, either urine or feces. The moister and more fly-congested it is, with a high concentration of smell, the less time has passed since it was left. Conversely, the more dehydrated and less fly-congested it is, with less concentration of smell, the longer it has been since the excretion. To obtain a more exact knowledge of the range of details, time it and analyze it in your laboratory (later in this chapter). In cold to freezing conditions, cut in half or open the feces. The inner moisture and heat will tell you its freshness. (Yes, it's a dirty job, but just remember: If it smells like it and looks like it, you surely do not have to taste it!)

LIVING CREATURES AND PLANT LIFE

Here, again, knowledge of the flora (plant life), fauna (wildlife), and insects of your immediate surroundings is paramount to success. In your climatic and geographic region of the world, knowing when certain species of animals come out to feed and at what time insects are the most active will certainly provide a clue as to the time a Chase traveled through the area.

For instance, most deer travel to water to drink during the late evening. If, during the dead of night or the crack of dawn, you notice a fresh deer's hoofprint in the middle of your Chase's shoe print, you can conclude with fair accuracy that the deer arrived after the Chase. If, however, your Chase's shoe print is superimposed on a deer's hoofprint, you can almost conclusively determine that the Chase was there after the deer. If the deer of the area normally go to the water source between approximately 8:00 p.m. and 9:00 p.m., and your team notices a fresh human footprint over the deer print at 11:30 p.m., the team can pretty safely assume that the Chase is a mere 2.5 to 3.5 hours ahead—or less.

Figure 5.1 Spiderweb.

Another example is a spider, which constructs a web during the late evening to capture late-flying insects (see figure 5.1). These webs are often strung along narrow trails that are wide enough to capture flying insects yet close enough from one side to the other to make the web construction quick and easy. If the Chase's prints are discovered in the early morning below a newly created spiderweb, the Tracker can assume that the Chase had passed through the area prior to the late evening of the day before.

Earthworm cast is another clear indicator of recent travel. Now, I am by no means a worm expert. I could dazzle you with Latin names such as Oligochaeta, *Lumbricus terrestris,* and Lumbriculida, all part of the worm population known as "segmented worms," but unless you are a pathologist or biologist, all you need to know is that worms are slimy and soft. Some earthworms are short, some are long, some are skinny, and some are fat. I have yet to see a pretty one.

A fact well known to many anglers, worms appear on the surface of the ground after rainfall or at predawn for air. As they travel, they simultaneously leave a mound or trail of moist mud pellets, called "worm cast." In tropical or subtropical regions of Southeast Asia, worm cast takes place between one and six o'clock in the morning, climate determining the exact hours it appears. Earthworms are not too fond of sunlight; therefore, before dawn, they return to their sweet, cool mother earth. A trail of worm cast that has been crushed by a human boot was most likely disturbed after those hours, indicating a more recent passage (see figures 5.2A and B). Conversely, footprints covered by a trail or mound of worm cast most likely occurred before 1:00 a.m. (see figures 5.3A, B, and C). For more information about these creatures, ask your local hard-core fishers. They will be able to tell you most anything you care to know—and some information you would rather not—about earthworms in your neck of the woods.

In the Pacific Northwest there are particular species of belly-crawlers known as slugs. They are similar to snails except that they have no shell and are extremely slimy. During the night and predawn hours, they come out to feed on new, tender plants, much to the dismay of area gardeners and florists. Slugs leave a very distinct trail of gelatinous ooze that dries and hardens with the sun. When disturbed, the appearance of the trail will tell you if it was smeared (while still moist) or broken (after it dried). This clue, of course, will give you a good indication of when the Chase traveled through the area.

The possibilities of these kinds of examples are nearly endless, limited only by one's knowledge of the animals, plants, and insects of a geographic area. Because this book is merely an overview, I do not have the luxury of examining the habitat and living habits of every possible living creature. There are other ways, however, to discover for yourself how the passage of time affects objects common to inhabitants of certain regions, while giving you the firsthand observation required of the most experienced Tracker.

One way is to go out with a seasoned Tracker, watching, smelling, touching, and listening as he or she explains the variances of signs according to the amount of time that has passed. Few novice Trackers have that kind of opportunity.

Another way to learn about the passage of time is much more scientific, for those of you who are analytically minded and/or have the patience to watch time unfold before your eyes. This method has greatly aided me in determining the age of various signs and has enabled me to build a detailed and highly accurate Tracker Analysis Database. It consists of an actual controlled laboratory test conducted in the outdoors over

Figure 5.2A Mound of worm cast—undisturbed.

Figure 5.2B Same worm cast—crushed by boot.

Figure 5.3A Worm cast—beginning traces.

Figures 5.3B Worm cast—closer view.

Figure 5.3C Worm cast—full night's work.

a predetermined period of time, during which you can actually watch, observe, and note the changes that affect both natural and objects.

CONTROLLED LABORATORY TEST

A controlled test is a systematic or logical procedure for judging the age of a sign. It will allow you to see firsthand how common objects and natural signs age and change over time. The setup is quite simple, and the experiment follows methods normally used in a typical scientific study.

The first and most important requirement is to find a secluded location that will not be disturbed by people or by animals outside the range of the experiment, such as dogs, cows, or other domesticated animals. Select a spot in an area where you would most likely be tracking someone, but protect it in such a manner that it will not be victim to acts of vandalism. If you want to be able to read the signs of the animals natural to the area, however, then avoid high fences or barriers that cannot be jumped or breached by native animal and insect inhabitants. The second requirement is to find a location that has both exposed and covered areas.

Depending on which type of climate you live in, divide the area into sections that equal the number of seasons you experience. If you live in an area that has only a wet and dry season, divide the area into two sections; if you live in a temperate climate with four distinct seasons, divide your laboratory into four sections. Then further divide each section into two compartments. One compartment should be exposed to the elements, to permit the full impact of sun, rain, snow, wind, and other weather phenomena. The other compartment should be under the natural cover of trees, bushes, or other plant life (see figure 5.4).

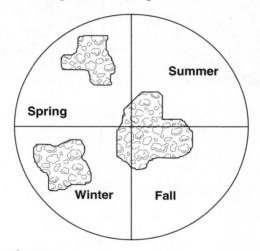

Figure 5.4 Combined test area.

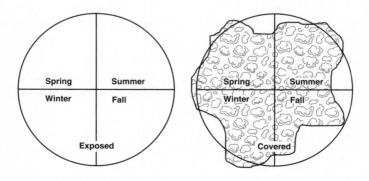

Figure 5.5 Divided test area—sheltered and unsheltered.

Depending on the abundance or lack of wide-open spaces or natural cover, you may find it easier to cordon off the exposed and covered areas first and then divide those areas into the two or four seasonal compartments (see figure 5.5).

The contents of each compartment will hold a wide variety of natural and man-made objects and should cover the spectrum of what you would expect to find during the course of a routine hunt or search and rescue operation. They should contain anything you would like to observe throughout the aging process, including but not limited to: a variety of cut plants abundant for each season; cut and scratched trees of many varieties; broken twigs; a campfire; shoe and/or boot prints made by adults and children, male and female, with a heavy pack and with no load at all; feces and urine; trash, such as newspapers, candy wrappers, food/soda/beer cans, cigarette butts, toilet paper, matchsticks; and food. Every attempt should be made to secure items that could be blown away, either by tacking them or tying them down.

Conduct of the Experiment

For each season, you will be setting up two compartments at a time, one sheltered, the other exposed to the elements, each containing identical items. The sheltered compartment should utilize a natural canopy of trees (building a shelter would defeat the purpose of observing the items in a natural setting). Put together the compartments during the peak of each season. In North America, throughout the majority of the United States, for example, the peak of spring would be May 10; summer would be July 10, and so on. For the tropics of Southeast Asia, the wet season is May to October, while the dry season is November to April. The peaks would be halfway through both seasons.

Build each individual sign in its most natural state, as it would naturally happen. Create a genuine atmosphere for your items, including, as I already mentioned, a natural canopy for your sheltered items. If replicating a Chase at rest, don't just sit on the ground for one minute and then use this as an actual illustration of a resting person. You would be wasting your time and fooling yourself. Take off a heavy pack, drop it to the ground, plop down beside it, and stretch your feet out, munching on a candy bar or eating a meal for ten to thirty minutes. Or rearrange the pack and use it as a pillow, then lie down and take a nap for an hour or overnight. Crumple the candy wrapper and throw it down. Walk through some tall grass, mud, and sand; run through some trees or brush, breaking, tearing, or scratching bark, leaves, branches, or exposed roots; climb a short rise; splash across some water. Even when urinating, do so as you would naturally, with males standing and women squatting.

Let your imagination, time, and area of availability be your guide. Just remember to do each of these things twice, once for the covered area and once for the exposed area in each seasonal compartment.

I have already mentioned that one of the things that set early American Trackers apart was their ability to tell the race, tribe, or home region of an individual by examining their excrement or their horses' droppings, as did Poor Elk in chapter 1. This next section will help you recognize characteristics that will let you do the same.

What You Eat Is What You Leave

Animals that live in a particular habitat or migrate from one geographic area to another on a seasonal, instinctual, or survival basis can be identified by their scat. It can also be said that a particular nationality or region of people can be identified by their excrement.

Now that the world is a "smaller place," imports and exports of food allow an individual to maintain a near exact diet to that of his home country or region, though he may be halfway around the world. In the same way, food from other countries can change the eating habits of domestic people, as will traveling to a foreign country and eating the foods of the local nationals. If you were to travel to Thailand and eat ethnic Thai food, your excrement would be the same as that of native Thai people. If three people from three different countries were to eat the exact same food and beverages in proportion to their capable intake, the excrement of each would be the same, as long as the three had been acclimated to the region in which they were eating. Hence, a human's excrement is a direct reflection of diet after digestion.

In order to get a good feel for what the excrement of three different diets might look like, I have devised an experiment that you can utilize within the compartments you have already set up. If you conduct the experiment correctly, your own waste products should look very similar to the photos I have included here.

Week One

Diet: Primary—Salmon, venison, nuts
                Fruit—Black/blueberries
                Beverage—water
Excrement: Residue of undigested nuts, berry seeds
                Color—mid to dark brown
                Appearance—moist yet rigid, segmented (see
                figure 5.6A)

Week Two

Diet: Primary—Trout, sardines, small grain rice
                Fruit and Vegetables—Tropical fruit, consisting of
                partially ripe mangoes, ripe papaya, ripe bananas,
                kiwi; mushrooms
                Beverage—Coconut milk with water, tea
Excrement: Residue of undigested papaya fiber, mango,
                and mushroom
                Color—light brown
                Appearance—moist and soft (see figure 5.6B)

Week Three

Diet: Primary—Chicken, oil, vinegar
                Fruit and Vegetables—tomatoes, carrots, celery,
                cucumbers, lettuce; peaches, oranges, nectarines
                Beverage—water, carrot juice
Excrement: Residue of undigested cucumber seeds
                Color—dark brown
                Appearance—moist, very rigid and segmented
                (see figure 5.6C)

This diet should be followed exactly for three straight weeks. To obtain the same results I have shown here, you must eat the exact same foods and drink the same beverages. Start each new diet at dinner/supper time, drinking plenty of water to flush out the last diet's excrement. Wait until the third result of your excrement or just prior to commencing the next diet, to get the best result of the entire week's intake. This will allow

Figure 5.6A Week One (human waste).

Figure 5.6B Week Two (human waste).

Figure 5.6C Week Three (human waste).

your body to fully process what you have eaten during the week and will give the best reflection of your diet's excrement.

Enjoy your meals, and don't forget to deliver your "product" into your test area(s) to examine the effects of time and weather.

Once you have set up your sites, analyze them over a period of five days, and then weekly thereafter until the peak of the following season. You *must* make copious notes, take pictures, and/or draw detailed sketches to aid your recall of what you have observed.

Initially, you may want to make note of hourly changes: How soon does the trampled grass stand back up? At what point does the sap of scratched or cut trees start to ooze, stop oozing, and change color? When do the leaves of broken branches start to wither? How soon is a bitten-into apple covered in ants and/or flies? What does a muddy print look like after an hour of sun? At what point do the edges start to dry out and lose their sharpness? Do whatever is necessary to aid your memory.

As your senses are aggressively probing the area, make note of the sticks, twigs, leaves, and grasses that have been bent, broken, crushed, bruised, or cut, thus making nature bleed as a rubber tree does. In the area of impact where nature's "flesh" has been exposed to the outside elements, discoloration will take place. A good example of this is an apple after it has been bitten into. The exposed area turns brown from oxidation. A bleeding tree is comparable to an individual who has been cut. Assuming the person is not a hemophiliac, his blood begins to coagulate and darken in color, soon becoming a scab. A rubber tree bleeds a white substance called *latex.* Latex stops leaking within two hours. Eight hours later, it hardens. After an additional twelve hours, the originally white latex changes to a dark brown. Fallen latex leaves (deadfall) will begin to turn brown within three days.

How does understanding the cause and effect of flora breached from its serenity aid you? Let's take the rubber tree as an example. You have been on a chase for two days. You have noticed that your Chase has set a pattern of using a sharp object to cut trees. On this occasion, you have come across a rubber tree that has been cut; the latex is whitish-beige in color and semi-hard. Based on the above information or experience, you can safely assume that it has been approximately six hours since the cut was made.

Prior knowledge of how flora responds to various human disturbances will be advantageous for comparison, but even without that knowledge, you can make an on-site comparison. If a tree is secreting sap, attempt to make a mirror-type incision on the same type of tree. If the flow of the sap is of equal speed, then you can say that it has not been long since this incision. But if the flow of sap is slower than the newly bruised or cut tree, you can say that the original incision has not been recently made.

Some flowers release an odor when torn or broken. If you encounter a plant that has recently been injured and the affected area has not changed color, go and smell the plant. (Note: It is important that you blow your nose before sampling the smells of various items. You need to obtain the genuine potency of the odor or fragrance.) If there is an odor or pleasant fragrance, attempt to create the same bruise or abrasion on the same type of plant—then smell it. The duller the odor of the original specimen, the older the injury and vice versa.

One example of this is a plant I have often encountered in the Caribbean, Central America, and Southeast Asia. *Mimosa pudica* is one of 1,700 species of the Leguminosa family. This particular plant can be found in tropical and subtropical environments, and it usually flourishes in open fields. It has shoots with sensitive, bipinated leaves with four secondary stalks and auxiliary tight clusters of flowers (see figure 5.7). The leaflets of this plant close during the night and open at sunrise, much like the morning glory does in the United States. Very sensitive to touch, it closes whenever it comes in contact with human fingers or other foreign objects (see figure 5.8); light rain will not close it. Only the portion that has been affected will actually close. If touched during the coolness of the morning, between the hours of 6:00 and 8:00, it will take up to thirty minutes for the bipinated leaves to open, depending on the heaviness of the dew. Between the hours of 8:00 a.m. and 10:00 a.m., it will take approximately twenty minutes for the leaves to reopen. If touched during the height of day, with the dryness and heat, it will be only three to five minutes before the plant reopens. And as the evening comes to a close with no dew in the coolness of the twilight, it takes ten to twenty minutes to reopen. Those plants growing under a canopy will experience a slight delay in the process of opening.

Therefore, knowing such things about the flora in your area will help you become much more competent in estimating the passage of time.

Back at the lab site, watch various activities come to pass as time goes on. Note when the animal life feeds, sleeps, and travels through your sites.

Figure 5.7 Mimosa pudica, *open.*

Figure 5.8 Mimosa pudica, *closed.*

Watch and listen for the insects and spiders to make their presence known. Record the times when the dewfall starts and ends. And pay close attention to the weather and its immediate and long-term effects on the objects in your lab. This analysis, carefully studied, will give your senses a full flavor of how time and the elements affect your lab items in a natural setting.

At the peak of the following season, set up the second pair of sites (covered, uncovered). Carefully analyze the first set of sites, and then construct the second. Repeat this process for every successive season until all seasons have been covered and all seasonal sites have been completed.

Most important, once you have set up the sites, do not touch or sanitize them in any way throughout the entire observation period. If you forget to include a certain item, be sure and insert it at the second location during the next season's setup.

At the earliest stage, it is important that you develop a systematic Tracker analysis report, using the art of observation and comparison. A critical comparison of a specific object must be performed in detail. Carefully observe the changes in individual objects as they change over time; notice the differences between the two sets of signs from one season to the next, noting the similarities and differences between the same objects in the two different sections. What color is the candy wrapper? How much did it deteriorate? Did the apple completely decompose, did it simply dry out, or did animals and/or insects accelerate the decomposition? How badly did the food can rust, if at all? Is there even the smallest indication of a footprint or travel through the site?

What about the cut tree? While some trees simply bruise, other trees "bleed" some kind of sap, latex, or other substance similar to syrup. Note the length of time it takes for the tree to stop bleeding or leaking. How long did it take to coagulate? To darken in color? How much time passed before it scabbed over and hardened?

What does a broken reed look like? Does a cut or broken flower emit an odor or fragrance? How long does it last or remain potent? Does the juice from the stem sting the hand or eyes and for how long? If a skunk has defended its territory with its strong spray, how long does the odor linger, how great a territory does it cover, and which plants hold on to the odor the longest?

Just keep in mind that for each geographical area, you will need to commit a full year to study it thoroughly.

Database

You must now create your database. This information will be such that you will refer back to it time and time again, especially when you are having difficulty judging the age of a particular item. It is imperative that it be as accurate as humanly possible. Remember, however, that the database is only good in the geographic region in which it was created. Don't expect the data from an arid region to be the same as that from a wet or cold region.

The look of the database can be whatever is the easiest for you to work with. Every time you make an observation of each Aging Stance make a Laboratory Observation Report for your database (see appendix E "Laboratory Observation Report").

Don't be shy about coming up with your own scenarios once you have started analyzing your findings. Remember the example of the rubber tree. If it has been cut and secretes latex that is whitish-beige in color, we know that this tree was cut approximately six hours earlier. I have spent a great deal of time in Southeast Asia. If I find fresh worm cast within the confines of a shoe print at 8:00 a.m., I can generally say without reserve that the shoe print was made between the hours of 1:00 a.m. and 6:00 a.m.

Similarly, in North America, you have noted that the majority of wildlife moves at night. If a white-tailed deer's print is superimposed over a person's footprint, you can assume that the individual moved through the area some time prior to the previous night.

Better yet, come up with a multifactor scenario, such as the one below.

The hour is 7:30 a.m., you are walking on a trail, and you notice the following signs:

1. Spiderwebs at a man's height have been torn apart; they are yellow in color.

2. Fresh flowing sap of a whitish-beige color is oozing from a rubber tree.

3. Fresh worm cast has been crushed by a shoe print.

What does this tell you? The torn spiderwebs could indicate that someone passed through the area between late evening and early morning (the yellow color indicates a new web); the flowing sap from the rubber tree indicates that the incision was made within a two-hour period; and the crushed worm cast (laid between 1:00 a.m. and 6:00 a.m.) indicates the shoe print was made after the break of dawn.

All three indicators taken together conclude that the shoe print was made about two hours earlier, at about 5:30 a.m. Better keep your eyes peeled and your rifles loaded if it is a dangerous Chase you are after.

A LESSON IN FORENSIC SCIENCE

There is yet another way to determine the passage of time, but it is not one I recommend that you include in your outdoor laboratory. Here, book studies and/or college classes will have to suffice. This, of course, is the study of forensic pathology, or the study of dead bodies.

Corpses tell us much about the amount of time that has elapsed since death, because each one passes through very distinct stages. The postmortem interval, or PMI, involves a predetermined set of steps that a decaying body experiences from the time of death to complete decomposition. This happens in four phases: rigor mortis, or stiffening of the body; putrefaction, which is the rotting of the body tissue; swelling or bloating of the entire body; and decomposition of the flesh, to the point at which all that remains are primarily bones.

There are three natural processes that occur in the body after death, and the extent of their development are clues to the estimated time of death. Algor mortis refers to the change in body temperature. The body temperature of a corpse will drop, equilibrating with the environment and reaching its peak in approximately ten to twelve hours at normal room temperature (about seventy to seventy-five degrees Fahrenheit). In the outdoors, higher temperatures may slow down cooling, and cold weather may speed it up. Livor mortis, also called "lividity," is the discoloration of the body that develops after the heart stops and no longer pumps blood through the body. You can see livor mortis approximately one hour after death, but it is often apparent earlier, within twenty to thirty minutes, usually becoming fixed in about eight to ten hours. This is the dark, deoxygenated blood pooling in parts of the body closest to the ground, and it is clearly evident as a purple color in a light-skinned person. On dark-skinned individuals, it will appear darker or may not be visible at all. Loss of blood before death will also lessen the appearance of lividity, while certain causes of death, such as carbon monoxide poisoning, cyanide poisoning, and hypothermia often cause the skin to appear bright red or pink.[17]

Rigor mortis, as mentioned above, refers to the stiffening of the body that begins shortly after death and sets in approximately one hour after death. The process starts at the head, moves down the body, and finally acts upon the legs and feet last, causing boardlike stiffness. This time-line, however, can be somewhat misleading, according to Dr. Dung Xuan Nguyen. Though it is well accepted that the jaw stiffens within an hour after death, complete rigor mortis could take as long as twelve hours. The process starts to occur within thirty minutes and takes up to twelve hours to reach its full term.[18]

A more exact PMI timeline of this first stage can be found in *Time of Death, Decomposition and Identification* by Jay Dix and Michael Graham. Although the exact time of death cannot be determined unless witnessed, there is normally sufficient evidence on the body itself to reach a close estimate, especially within the first twelve hours after death has occurred.

Beyond these initial stages of decomposition, the time interval between each successive stage depends entirely upon the climatic conditions surrounding the corpse. Is it located in an aquatic (water) or terrestrial (land) environment? Is its surface completely exposed, or has it been buried partially or totally? What kind of carnivore, insect, or rodent activity has taken place since death? How large is the body and what type of clothing was worn by the individual?

....

17 Jay Dix and Michael Graham, *Time of Death, Decomposition and Identification* (Boca Raton, Florida: CRC Press, 2000), 6, 4–5.

18 Dr. Dung Xuan Nguyen, interview with the author, June 2000. Dr. Dung was a surgical doctor during the Vietnam War, served approximately two years in a Communist reeducation camp in North Vietnam, and now works in Washington State as a general practitioner.

Decomposition

By far the most influential factor on decomposition is temperature.[19] Tropical, subtropical, and/or warm climates expedite the growth of the bacteria that cause decomposition. In the South Pacific and Asia, studies give us a glimpse of decomposition time intervals in the tropics. For example, in Sri Lanka, an island off the coast of India, putrefaction can occur within twenty-four hours; swelling of the whole body can happen within sixty to seventy-two hours. A body exposed to direct sunlight and outdoor heat may decompose within a twenty-four- to forty-eight-hour period, at which time visual identification is nearly impossible.[20]

Subfreezing areas, on the other hand, preserve bodies for long periods of time. Note recent discoveries of centuries-old mammoths and "ice men."

Mummification

Ancient Egyptians perfected the science of mummification, giving us the age-old fodder for classic novels and Friday-night thrillers. But mummification can occur naturally, too—arid deserts also preserve bodies in this way. Dix and Graham provide an excellent description of the natural mummification process:

> *Mummification occurs in hot dry environments where the body is able to dehydrate and bacterial proliferation is minimal. The skin becomes dark, dry and leathery. The internal organs desiccate and shrink. Most mummification occurs in the summer months but may also occur during the winter if the temperature is warm enough. An entire body can mummify in a few days to weeks. As the skin dries and hardens, the soft tissues decompose. After a few weeks, an entire body may appear preserved with some shrinkage due to dehydration. If, however, an incision is made through the skin, soft tissues, fat and*

19 Debra A. Kumar, "Decay Rates in Cold Climates: A Review of Cases Involving Advanced Decomposition from the Examiners Office in Edmonton, Alberta, Canada," *Journal of Forensic Science* 43.1 (January 1998): 57–61.

20 Dirk H. R. Spenneman and Franke Bernd, "Decomposition of Buried Human Bodies and Associated Death Scene Materials on Coral Atolls in the Tropical Pacific," *Journal of Forensic Science* 40.3 (May 1995): 356–67.

internal organs may be virtually absent with the body resembling a "bag of bones." Once the body is in this state, it may remain preserved for many years unless the skin is torn or broken. Mummification localized to certain parts of the body is relatively common. Mummification of the fingers and toes occurs readily in relatively dry environments regardless of temperature.[21]

Skeletonization

Complete skeletonization also depends on environmental factors. According to a study conducted by the University of Tennessee, in moderate climates a body will usually decompose down to just skeletal remains within six weeks during the summer and within four months in the winter cold. Of course, this time interval is significantly accelerated "when postmortem animal activity" speeds up the process.[22]

I have included here two medical examiner's charts that approximate the time of death according to specific bodily changes (see figures 5.9A and B). This should assist in the time interval identification from rigor mortis to adipocere (a waxy substance that accumulates on the fatty parts of the body; it may protect a corpse from decomposition).

• • •

As with other signs noted by experienced Trackers, the study of forensic pathology offers clues regarding the actual passage of time. Aging, whether estimating the time of a person's death or determining how long ago a footprint was left, is not something that can be learned overnight or after a couple of trips out in the wilderness. The serious tracking student will use all available means to learn about the age of signs, including one-on-one instruction, reading, and hands-on experimentation. As is true with nearly all factors of tracking, this skill, too, relies heavily on experience before an individual can truly become an accomplished Tracker.

....

21 Dix and Graham, 13–14.

22 Kumar, 57–61.

Stage	Description	Freshwater Time	N	Seawater Time	N
Fresh	Absence of significant discoloration or bloating; rigor mortis and livor mortis may be present	0–2 days	38	0–3 days	22
Early decomposition	Significant discoloration and early to full bloating	2 days–1 week	11	2 days–1 week	4
Advanced decomposition	Beginning of adipocere development; sagging and bleaching of soft tissue; erosion of surface tissue	1 week–1 month	13	?	2
Skeletonization	Exposure of skeletal elements; often significant adipocere development	1 month or longer	1	?	1

Reprinted with permission from *Forensic Taphonomy: The Postmortem Fate of Human Remains,* Copyright CRC Press, Boca Raton, Florida.

Figure 5.9A Table 1 Stages of Decay, Criteria for Classification, Duration of Time in the Water and Sample Size for Seawater and Freshwater Cases

Time after Death	Postmortem Changes	Modifiers	Category	Stage
0 minutes	Circulation and breathing stop Pallor Early lividity Muscular relaxation Sphincters may relax	Temperature Humidity Outdoor location Indoor location Submerged in water	Early changes	
2 hours	Vascular changes in eye Rigor mortis begins Algor mortis begins Lividity easily seen		Late changes	
4–5 hours	Coagulation of blood Fixation of lividity			
24 hours	Drying of cornea Reliquefication of blood		Putrid Tissue changes	I II
48 hours	Rigor disappears Intravascular hemolysis			III
72 hours	Loss of hair and nails			
96 hours	Skin slippage and bulla formation Bacterial overgrowth	Insect activity Animal activity	Bloated	IV V
Days-months	Green discoloration Bloating Release of gases Release of liquified internal organs Gradual loss of soft tissues Partial skeletonization Complete skeletonization	Mummification Adipocere formation	Destruction Skeleton	VI VII VIII XI X

Reprinted with permission from *Forensic Taphonomy: The Postmortem Fate of Human Remains,* Copyright CRC Press, Boca Raton, Florida.

Figure 5.9B Table 2 Postmortem Changes

THE PURSUIT: DAY THREE

Before leaving the relative security of the hilltop, the team members reapply camouflage; eject, retrieve, and wipe dry the chambered rounds from their weapons; reload new rounds to prevent possible misfire; double-check their equipment; and make sure they are ready for any encounter that may take place during the day.

Major Kim approaches Jordan. "Please ensure that the civilian is not harmed."

Jordan addresses his concern. "Major, the civilian is not my worry. My men know the difference between combatants and noncombatants. Target recognition is well ingrained in their training. It's you I am worried about. I'm sure you are a great soldier, but we have never trained together. Follow our lead. Once we have dominated, captured, and/or neutralized our targets, then you can safeguard and reassure the noncombatant."

Samoa takes a few minutes to peer through binoculars in all directions once the first rays of dawn lighten the sky. He neither sees anyone nor hears anything from the team's hill to surrounding ridges or down into the valleys, except the sights and sounds common to the small farms dotting the region.

O'Connor takes the primary Tracker position this morning to give Badilla a longer break and to ensure that the team medic is not on point when eventual contact is made. Following a sudden change in direction, they head southwest, going down a finger, and then crossing the Hun Chiang Stream. They continue in this direction for another half kilometer, when O'Connor comes across fresh pointers, indicating downhill movement.

He leads them across the Yeong Chiang Stream, and shortly thereafter he notices a quick change in direction up the hill to their left. He signals a quick halt and immediate silence, as the team drops and takes cover. Their Chase may have discovered the pursuit of their detachment and taken to the hill to put up a strong defense. Although the signs are still at least eight hours old, there is no way to tell whether or not the infiltrators are still there, in dug-in positions, ready for a fight.

Badilla immediately takes over as both point man and Tracker as the team uses the bounding overwatch to advance up the hill. The detachment splits up into two teams, one on either side of the trail, taking turns moving as Badilla stays with the lead team to identify any booby traps or possible ambush sites.

At the top of the hill, the first team discovers no infiltrators, and the detachment comes together as Badilla moves into an area dotted with four flattened sites. He sees the same pattern of pancaking as he did the day before, indicating four people sitting in all-around security. Near one of the flattened spots, there appears to be a cooking area. Within a half-meter patch of ground, he discovers three smaller circles of heat-yellowed grass, small amounts of rice, and garlic skin. But here he finds something else—rope marks on six of the trees in the immediate vicinity of three of the flattened sites. Upon completion of his pattern, he makes his notes and returns to the team.

"I think it's pretty clear that there are four people in this group," Badilla explains. "Four clearly defined sitting areas and what appears to be a cooking area, with one person doing the cooking. I found pieces of rice and garlic within that zone, so my guess is that they are of Asian origin."

Major Kim cautions that they could be making it appear that they are Asian. They could just as easily be Middle Eastern professionals eating native food to better blend in with the local populace.

"Either way, three of them are using hammocks." Badilla smiles. "They must be pretty comfortable in their security if they feel they have the luxury of stringing hammocks. Of course, our unfortunate civilian appears to have spent the night on the ground. The rope marks are very fresh, as if they were pulled off the trees in a big hurry. And I found a number of small signs that may indicate they left rather quickly." He points toward the trail they have just come off. "It looks like they headed back toward the trail no more than an hour ago. We could have come close to a surprise meeting if we hadn't come up this way."

Jordan immediately calls back to the base camp to report their whereabouts and possible imminent contact. He requests the teams that have been shadowing them on either side to move in closer for possible support during the firefight. Then he turns to the team members and relays rendezvous points and contingency plans to be used for the next three hours.

In a careful hurry, the team follows the fresh trail downhill, Badilla noting fresh waist-high pointers on the way down and fresh boot prints near the stream. Upon closer examination of one of the prints, Badilla concludes that it is the same print he saw the day before at the Yeong Chiang crossing. He relays to Jordan through O'Connor that the print is thirty minutes or less old.

Jordan orders a parallel pursuit, and the team moves south of the trail in imminent contact formation. Major Kim moves closer to the detachment commander to provide immediate translation of whatever is said.

In front, Badilla drops to his knee. Instinctively the other team members drop in unison, as if they were not five, but one person. With his non-shooting hand, he points with his index finger fully extended, his thumb pointing down in the signal of enemy at his direct front. He then follows that by holding up three fingers, then five, indicating three infiltrators five meters away. Without a noise, they move into covered and concealed positions.

The tallest, a distinct Korean in an Adidas fleece sports outfit and appearing to be the person in charge, stops suddenly and looks in the direction of the team, apparently seeing nothing. He begins barking orders, and the Koreans scatter. One grabs a slightly built local civilian dressed in jeans and a heavy sweater and pulls him behind a tree. Another dives behind a rock, while the leader dashes away from both groups, pulling wire from his equipment belt.

In an urgent whisper, Major Kim translates what he hears to Jordan. "They are going to kill the civilian and set a booby trap!"

Jordan signals a staggered attack with individual immediate action drills.

Badilla rises and emerges from behind a pine tree, when three rounds are fired from a silencer weapon. Two whiz by his left ear, and the other grazes his right forearm. Without hesitation,

O'Connor avenges Badilla's flesh wound by delivering a "Mozambique"—two shots to the chest and one to the head—at the one who injured his partner.

As the North Korean falls limp, three canisters of highly concentrated white smoke fill the area between the two groups to cover the infiltrators' break in contact. As soon as the dead Korean falls, the mushroom picker takes advantage of the distraction and starts yelling in the Hangul Mal Korean language.

Major Kim shouts at Jordan as shots fire in the air. "Don't shoot at the yelling man! He says he is but a farmer!"

"If he's not a threat, he won't be shot!" Jordan assures him.

O'Connor turns his head slightly and yells back. "Samoa, move!"

To protect the initial assault team and keep the enemy's heads down, both Badilla and O'Connor lay a heavy volume of suppressive fire, while Samoa and the rest of the team move forward quickly by fire and maneuver, remaining ever aware of the enemy's booby traps and their own interval.

As Rowe crosses his sector and approaches the civilian, the old man continues to yell, his hands still bound behind him. His frantic movements indicate that there is no booby trap attached to his body. Rowe grabs him and tells him to be quiet, his tone of voice crossing all language barriers. The Korean farmer immediately falls silent. After Rowe finishes sweeping the small objective, Major Kim approaches the old man, cutting the tight ropes, which have already discolored his hands, and replacing them with plastic flex-cuffs on his hands and feet.

Samoa whistles a signal for O'Connor and Badilla to make the cross-sweep over the danger area. Halfway across, Badilla nears the fallen infiltrator. In a nerve twitch, the Korean's hand moves as if toward his weapon. Badilla double-taps him on the chest, immediately seeing the ignited fuse. "Booby trap!"

O'Connor rushes to Badilla's side, yanks open his first-aid pouch, and cuts the two-minute fuse with his surgical scissors, amazed that the North Korean soldier managed to ignite the fuse before his death.

Badilla and Rowe search the dead body as the rest of the team consolidates, reorganizes, and gives Samoa the ACE (Ammunition, Casualty, and Equipment) report. Jordan orders that the booby trap be blown in place to make the infiltrators think the claymore mine went off as planned. Then they continue on with the pursuit. While the booby trap is being detonated, Rowe calls in a SALUTE report with details about the location of the farmer, still an unknown, and the body of the dead infiltrator for follow-on security patrols. By this time, the entire team has inserted a fresh thirty-round magazine into the magazine well of their M-4 carbines.

The unknown civilian is still pleading that he is merely a farmer, but the team has no choice but to treat him as a possible infiltrator disguised as a farmer. Major Kim believes in the old man's innocence and pleads his case to Jordan, but the detachment commander explains there is no time and he will be properly taken care of by the follow-on teams. The old man is treated humanely, though left tied to a tree as the team continues their pursuit.

Samoa looks toward Badilla, who has already put a pressure dressing on his forearm and is conducting the Tracker Observation Procedures, and gives the latter the thumbs-up signal to resume the chase.

The trail is easy and unobscured now, the fleeing infiltrators making no attempt to cover their trail. Within ten minutes, the signs of running are transformed to those of a more casual pace, the Chase evidently more confident after hearing the booby trap explode. The team spreads out, preparing for an envelopment.

Within fifteen minutes of reestablishing the chase, Badilla again signals the appearance of the enemy to his front. Although making haste, the two are walking, not running.

Jordan points to either side of the enemy, signaling the completion of the envelopment. Samoa and Rowe take a wide sweep to the right side of the infiltrators, Badilla and O'Connor doing the same on the left. Once they are in position, Jordan gives the signal to attack.

Shouts and gunfire erupt as the team rushes at the startled North Korean soldiers. Major Kim yells in Korean to surrender. The North Korean leader yanks a pistol from its holster and begins firing toward Samoa and Rowe. Jordan immediately ends the threat with well-aimed shots to the chest and head. As the Korean falls to the ground, the last infiltrator throws down her AK-47 and raises her hands, yelling frantically, "No shoot! No shoot!" The team surrounds her, weapons trained on her lest she make any false moves, and she is thoroughly searched before being cuffed and secured.

"Holy smokes!" Rowe exclaims as he and Major Kim finish the search of the dead leader. "Look at this!" He opens the leader's pack and shows a two-foot-long cylinder inscribed in Korean. "Tell them what it says, Major."

Major Kim nods. "It says, 'Chemical product of Kanggye and Sakchu factories.'"

"I've got true blue bugs in my hands, brothers!" Rowe shouts triumphantly.

Jordan shakes his head and looks back in the direction they have just come. "They were headed toward the water reservoir. Good job."

Within another ten minutes, US and Korean military forces link up with the tired but satisfied detachment. Jordan relinquishes command and control to them, turning over the captured infiltrator and recovered items to the appropriate teams. [Note: Later that day, the detachment learns that the infiltrator has bitten off her own tongue while being flown back to an interrogation site, just to keep from talking.]

The joint coalition commander shakes Jordan's hand, congratulating him on a job well done. Jordan refuses credit, pointing instead toward Samoa, Rowe, and the rest of the team. "We're just doing our job, sir."

At 1500 hours, Detachment 266 is extracted from the hills of Korea.

Mission complete.

CHAPTER 6

What Do We Have Here?

When speculation has done its worst,
two and two still make four.

—Samuel Johnson

In the last four chapters, we have discussed the essentials of tracking. We have learned how to identify a Chase, use our senses to find almost anyone, understand the effect of external factors on signs left behind, and determine the approximate age of a sign.

Now, if we harness all we have learned, we can gather a great deal of information about our Chase with the slightest clue. We can discover not only the age of a sign, which we discussed in chapter 5, but also the Chase's direction of movement; speed; number of people that comprise or are with the Chase; kind of food consumed; health, morale; comfort items utilized; and types of equipment and/or weapons carried.

GATHERING THE EVIDENCE

Information on your Chase is gathered in much the same way as a detective would gather evidence at a crime scene. And, likewise, before we can gather our information, we must preserve *our* version of the "crime scene."

Preserve the Area

The place in which the first sign is detected is the most critical of all such locations. Here you will make your first determination regarding the Chase's direction of travel, speed, distance ahead, numerical strength, and overall condition. Your initial action plan will be based on what is discovered about your Chase during this opening assessment—and in many cases you cannot afford to be wrong!

The initial search for that first sign may be incredibly easy, the sign blatantly displayed for all to see. On the other hand, finding that first sign may take the sharpest skills of the best Tracker. Either way, all team members must take exceptional care to keep from contaminating the initial search area.

Preservation of this scene is essential to your success. Do whatever is necessary to avoid contaminating the area until the initial search has been completed. With trained military and police Trackers, this does not normally cause a great deal of concern; these teams have been taught to watch, look, and listen before so much as taking a step in any direction. You must adopt the same practices, whether by yourself or with a team of searchers.

Once the first sign has been discovered, everyone involved in the search must stop and remain in place. Normally, if in a group, the first person to recognize a sign will give a verbal or nonverbal signal that can be clearly understood by all and interpreted to mean "freeze." Everyone must understand the ramifications of this action. In a hostile situation, the team takes on a security posture while the Tracker and coverman perform the appropriate Tracker Observation Procedure to reestablish the Chase's path. In a nonhostile situation, team members must still stop immediately, lest they accidentally step on a sign. Once a sign has been obliterated or contaminated, it can never be recovered. Critical pieces of evidence may be lost, which could have life-and-death consequences.

The people who should cause the most concern are the untrained and uninitiated. On a search and rescue mission, these may be the "Good Samaritans" who have come to help find little Johnny. With the most noble of intentions, they have little or no knowledge about how to conduct an initial search—and they easily contaminate the point at which the Chase was last seen. It is a classic case of good initiative but bad judgment. These are the people who are most likely to step on a boot print in the dirt, to sit on flattened grass, or to cut off a broken branch to use it as a walking stick.

As a professional, I am frustrated by their ignorance, but as a parent I fully understand their drive to do something—anything—to find their child or loved one. They do not intentionally set out to destroy life-saving evidence, but the result is just as devastating.

The same can be said for outside observers in a police chase or military operation. These may be reporters out to catch the "scoop" before their competition gets wind of the story; they may be explorer scouts participating in an expedition to earn points or badges; they may be supervisors or higher ranking authorities evaluating the actions of their subordinates; or they may be interpreters who speak the language of the Chase or the locals in the area of operation to ensure clarity of communication. Whoever these people are, they must be briefed on their responsibilities and be watched closely throughout the conduct of the operation.

If by chance the initial search area does get contaminated, the team will need to utilize the track casting drill found in the following chapter before commencing their efforts.

Direction of Movement

Once the initial scene has been preserved, the first thing the Tracker or tracking team must do is determine a generalized direction of travel. After tracking for a given distance, you will be able to establish the direction your Chase is going, assuming he has no other means of transportation but moving on the ground by foot. Let us also presume that fresh shoe prints were recently found. If these assumptions are correct, you should be able to establish a general cardinal direction (north, northeast, south, southwest, etc.). You have just succeeded in cutting the search direction from a sweeping 360-degree area circumference to a much narrower thirty- to forty-five-degree search corridor. This not only reduces the distance you will cover, but it also greatly reduces the time involved in finding the Chase.

Direction of travel is determined a number of different ways, as alluded to in the previous chapters. If you are fortunate enough to have a clear footprint, analyze it carefully. Don't automatically assume that the direction of the print is the direction of travel. Examine the print;

take notice of the deepest points, the weight distribution, and the space between the stride. The Chase may in fact be walking backward to deceive his pursuers! (See figures 6.1A and B.)

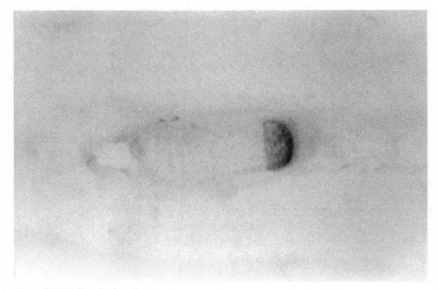

Figure 6.1A Walking backward.

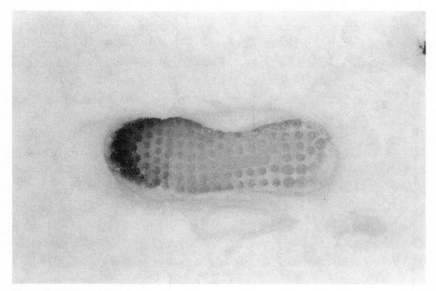

Figure 6.1B Walking forward.

Take a closer look at areas of flattened grass or tall grass trails. The tips of the reeds will point like fingers toward the Chase. Similarly, note the direction of other foliage that has been pancaked, brushed, bent, or broken; this also points in the direction of our Chase. These signs, appropriately, are known as "pointers" (see figure 6.2; also refer back to figures 4.18, 4.19, and 4.20). Branches broken and hanging down will still leave a telltale mark. At the point of the break, the portion hanging down should

Figure 6.2 Pointers.

be at least slightly cocked to one side or lightly twisted. See if you can tell which way the top of the leaves or needles are pointing. That is most likely the Chase's direction of travel. Spiderwebs can also serve as pointers, since they tend to break away from, but in the general direction of, he who tore it. Likewise, brushed-off moss from rocks, trees, or vines displaced from their natural state, or the transfer of mud from a wet to a dry area, are also clear indicators (see figures 6.3A and B; also refer back to figures 4.4B and 4.21).

Figure 6.3A Mud transfer.

Figure 6.3B Mud transfer.

Use your senses, as we discussed in chapter 3. Listen for sounds of a radio or chopping wood; pay close attention to the cessation of or sudden increase in insect sounds; watch for an explosive flocking of birds. Determine the wind direction, close your eyes, and take notice of whether or not you can smell smoke, kerosene, or cooking food. All of these will expose the Chase's direction of movement or the particular area in which he has set up camp.

If the Chase has a bleeding wound, he can also be tracked by his trail of blood.

Blood Trailing

Excreted blood examined at the point of impact will tell Trackers many things by its configuration and color, if they know what to look for. At this point, blood will be configured in one of four ways or a combination of the four, depending on the volume of flow, the vegetation, and the speed of the victim's movement. Blood will either be made up of smears or blots, splatters, puddles, or drops. This configuration, in combination with the color, can tell you volumes about your Chase's condition, types of wounds, and location of wounds.

Dark Red. Blood without oxygen is darker than that found in arteries. If the color of the blood at the point of impact is dark red, indicating a lack of oxygen, this usually means that the wound originated from a cut vein or a puncture. If untreated, the wound would emit a constant flow of blood, and you would see consistent smears and/or drops of blood in areas of heavy vegetation; more arid regions would reveal more drops on the ground and fewer smears.

Red. If the blood is bright red, indicating oxygenation, the wound most likely originated from an artery. The blood would flow in a regular, pulsating fashion, in keeping with the timing of the Chase's heartbeat. With this type of untreated wound, heavy vegetation would contain a combination of smears, drops, and splatters at regular but separated interval patterns.

Light Red. Perhaps you have come across a blood sample that is light red in color or has the appearance that it has been diluted or mixed with other fluids. In most cases, this would indicate an abdominal wound, since the blood has been mixed with gastric fluids, intestinal fluids, bile, urine, or bowel matter. These samples will also emit unpleasant odors. The pattern of blood from these wounds would be inconsistent, since they may flow irregularly. Bleeding from these wounds may occur either internally, externally, or both, due to the diversion of blood into, say, the abdominal cavity. External flow occurs when the fluids are suddenly released through the wound opening, either because the cavity has filled up and is overflowing, or because the Chase has exerted extra physical effort, bent over, or applied pressure near the wound.

Pink. Pinkish blood, which is usually foamy in appearance, indicates a chest wound resulting from a punctured lung, and is the result of the mixture of air, water, and oxygenated blood reacting with lung fluid. (Note: If the chest wound does not puncture the lungs, expect to see dark red or bright blood if an artery has been punctured.) Flow from these types of wounds would be slow, oozing, with the smears or drops undefined and bubbly in appearance. Many times, the blood fills up the chest first, then oozes from the wound. Blood found on foliage at chest level, on top of signs found at chest level, and/or on top of ground signs all may indicate the presence of a chest wound.

The pattern of the drops or droplets can also tell you the direction of travel. Because the fall of blood, as other liquids, is affected by the movement of the object or person it is released from, it rarely drops straight down. If you were to take a ball, walk down the street, and drop the ball, you would find that it would bounce in the direction you were traveling, notwithstanding any rocks or irregular objects it may hit upon impact. If you were running when you dropped the ball, it would bounce faster in the direction you were traveling. A similar thing happens with a drop of blood when it falls from a person. Now, obviously, blood doesn't bounce like a ball, so it has to make adjustments to account for the centrifugal force.

I'm sure everyone has seen the shape of a drop of water. In its absolutely natural state (say, in space or a vacuum bottle), it forms a perfect sphere, like a ball. As the forces of gravity take over, as in a raindrop falling to the ground, the lower end remains spherical in shape but the upper end is pulled into a cone shape. If the drop hits the ground from an exact perpendicular angle, it spreads out in a precise circle, with perhaps a few secondary splashes giving the circle an appearance similar to a circular saw blade. The higher the drop when it begins to fall, the more rugged the circle and the more pronounced the secondary splashes once it hits the earth. Now release the drop of water from a slowly moving object. The upper, cone-shaped end of the drop reacts to the movement and "flops over," pointing in the direction of travel once the drop hits the ground. If released from a person or object moving at a faster speed, the cone end of the drop spreads out even further. The same thing happens with a drop of blood.

To get a clear idea of what this would look like on a real pursuit, try this experiment. Purchase some imitation blood. (This can be found in "goulash kits," used by the medical profession for trauma case training, or you can purchase theater "blood" from a costume shop, which may be easier to come by near Halloween.) Although it is not exactly the same consistency as real blood, it is close enough to gain a good understanding of the falling patterns. (*Please* do not cut yourself to get the "real thing"!) Put it in an eyedropper, and find a flat piece of ground covered with a shiny, smooth surface (cement, tile, hardwood with no seams or cracks). Without otherwise moving, squeeze out a drop of "blood" from various heights, for instance, from ankle, knee, waist, chest, and head levels. Notice the pattern each drop leaves. Then do the same thing while walking slowly, walking at a fast pace, jogging, and running. Again, make note of the patterns you see. You should notice that the tip of the droplet points in your direction of travel; you should also notice that the tip becomes longer the faster your travel speed.

In order to etch these patterns into your memory, take pictures or draw sketches of the patterns at each height level and each speed you traveled. You may want to keep the photos or sketches in a notebook to which you can easily refer at a later date and time. For even greater accuracy, repeat this experiment on different kinds of terrain and in varying vegetation.

Keep in mind, however, that actual patterns will differ somewhat from what you saw above. For instance, blood from extremity wounds will not fall in a straight, precise line because of the action of walking. Normally when a person is walking, he swings his arms back and forth, opposite the placement of his feet. Immediately after the heel of the foot touches the ground, the foot holds that position for just a second. As a stride is about to take place, the foot rolls rhythmically onto the ball, then to the toes in order to maintain balance. Simultaneously, the opposite leg makes a forward motion.

Because of this motion, swinging hands and walking/running feet will cause the blood to be tossed and scattered forward and backward, and possibly smeared alongside the Chase's path. The drops falling from the backward swing will have the tip pointing in the *opposite* direction of travel, and this could confuse the untrained Tracker. Further observation should yield additional drops pointing in the actual direction of travel. Compare the two, and you will find that the drops pointing in the actual direction of travel will have longer tips than the ones dropped from a backward arm swing.

If the wound is in the upper torso at chest/lung height, blood will be found at chest level or on the ground, unless the Chase is stumbling or disoriented.

Also keep in mind that blood is subject to the obstacles that may be in its falling airborne path. This could include branches, rocks, equipment, shoes, and an infinite number of other objects that will affect the fall and the resulting pattern.

Speed of Movement

The second element a Tracker must determine is the Chase's travel speed, which will give you or the team an idea of how much time it will take you to overcome, catch up to, or close in on him. Let me give you some examples that demonstrate speed of movement under both optimum and typical tracking conditions.

In 1991, Artur Marrios of Mexico ran 13 miles, 197 yards in one hour. In 1998, Tegla Loroupe of Kenya achieved 11 miles, 697.4 yards in the same amount of time. They are the record-holders for longest distance covered in one hour.[23] These are admirable feats of human speed, and I salute their accomplishments. Without a doubt, these athletes trained for their events with hard work and strict discipline. But let's add thirty, seventy, even one hundred pounds to their backs, and let's say their paths were uneven, burdened by obstacles such as mangroves, deep snow, sand dunes, wadis, secondary jungles, or mountains. One doesn't have to be a physics major to conclude that their times would dramatically decrease.

Now let's look at the Appalachian Trail, which runs from Maine to Georgia and covers a distance of 2,100 miles (supposing the hiker doesn't go off course!). The hard-core "thru-hiker" averages 14.5 miles per day (both male and female) carrying a weight of thirty to seventy pounds. One survey found that the usual thru-hiker started at 7:30 a.m. and walked for ten hours per day. Some took a five- to ten-minute break every hour; others took approximately one half hour for lunch and made three ten-minute stops; all averaged a total of one hour per day break time, consumed by lunch, rest, snacking, views, and visiting with other hikers. Even with the steady pace and relatively light load, the average thru-hiker took 5.5 to 6 months to complete the challenging trail.[24]

The accomplishments of the Appalachian Trail thru-hikers are also admirable, as well as hazardous. But now let's look at the average ground force soldier.

A ground soldier must be ready to hit the ground in whatever place or climate he is ordered, whether acclimated or not. In his ruck (backpack) he will be carrying fifty to seventy pounds of gear from the Point of

23 *Guinness World Records 2003* (London: Guinness World Records, 2003), 258, 358.

24 Roland Mueser, *Long Distance Hiking, Lessons from the Appalachian Trail* (Camden, ME: Ragged Mountain Press, 1998), 83, 87, 85, 81.

Infiltration (departure from friendly lines) to the Objective Rallying Point (ORP—the last rendezvous point before assaulting the final objective). He is on a route that has been deliberately planned to give him, his team, and his unit the tactical advantage, at a speed of movement commensurate with the climate, geographic conditions, and probability of enemy contact (possible, probable, or imminent), as determined by intelligence reports and the leader's assessment of the situation. Speed will never violate security; the element of surprise must be maintained at all times. Once he reaches the ORP, his gear is cached and reduced to only that which is absolutely necessary to accomplish the mission, be it a raid, ambush, or other tactical maneuver. This usually means operational equipment, extra meals, and water that will sustain him until he returns to friendly lines or performs a follow-on mission. Let's say he retrieves ten pounds of sustainable equipment from his pack. In order to accomplish his mission, he must add his weapon, ammunition, night vision goggles, two quarts of water, survival gear, knife, first-aid kit, gas mask, grenades, smoke, and ballistics vest, all of which add at least an additional forty-five pounds.

Throughout my career in the Special Forces, I have learned that the average soldier carrying a fifty-pound pack has a thirty-inch step and travels at a normal pace of 106 steps per minute. I have also discovered that a typical soldier can move cross-country, carry fifty pounds for four to eight miles per day, and sustain this pace for four days. This includes meals, rest, sleep, and other stops; it does not take into consideration enemy action or reaction.

A US Army study calculated the average rate of movement on roads/ flat terrain, mountainous terrain, and cross-country, as follows:

1. Road/flat terrain: 4.0 kilometers per hour (kph), daytime; 3.2 kph, limited visibility.

2. Cross-country (rolling hills and vegetation): 2.4 kph, daytime; 1.6 kph, limited visibility.

3. Mountainous terrain, with extreme obstacles: ascent—300 meters per hour; descent—600 meters per hour.[25] (Note: This

25 "Mountain Operations," U.S. Army Field Manual 3–97.6: pages 4–7 and 4–8, figure 4–3.

will be even slower when dealing with high altitude, snow, glacial crevices, subzero temperatures, deadfall, and proper equipment/clothing.)

Other terrain can be calculated as follows:
Tropical rain forest: 1,000 meters per hour/1 kph.
Deciduous forest, secondary jungle, tall grass (3 to 5 meters tall): 500 meters per hour.
Mangroves and swamp: 100 to 300 meters per hour.
Rice paddies: wet—800 meters per hour; dry—2,000 meters per hour.
Plantations: 2,000 meters per hour.
Trails: 1,500 meters per hour.[26]

Now, let's put all this together and apply it to the tracking scenario. Using this information, calculate your speed compared to the speed of your Chase, using the age of the last sign left by the Chase. Do this at succeeding signs, and you will have a pretty clear indication about whether you need to pick up the pace or slow down (based on your objective).

Say, for instance, you are traveling 1,000 meters every 100 minutes (10 meters per minute); all signs are indicating that your Chase is maintaining a constant 3-hour-and-20-minute lead (200-minute lead). First, you are both traveling at approximately the same speed, but he has a 200-minute lead. If you double your speed to 20 meters per minute for 80 minutes, you will have effectively doubled your distance to 2,000 meters within the first 100 minutes. The Chase will now have only an 80-minute lead. At that point, you would decrease your velocity as your contact becomes probable to imminent, in order to maintain the element of surprise. (Never violate the number one principle of patrolling: security!)

Other factors will also contribute to the team's ability to close with and/or engage the Chase. External conditions will have an effect on the Chase's speed, either by stifling it or aiding movement. Sand, rough terrain, and heavy foliage will slow down the Chase's movement speed, while flat, open terrain will enhance his movements. Likewise, the weather conditions will also affect the Chase's speed of travel.

26 "Jungle Operations," U.S. Army Field Manual 90–5: page B-2.

123

Internal conditions, however, will also affect his speed. His physical health or conditioning will determine whether or not he can sustain a fast, steady pace; it will also determine the length of time he can sustain that pace. Likewise, the Chase's mental state will either assist or degrade his abilities to keep pushing ahead. While anger or fear releases adrenaline, often strengthening a person physically, depression or anxiety frequently weakens an individual.

A person's spiritual state can also affect his abilities to elude his pursuers. One who has a strong belief in God, Allah, or another higher power will generally be able to withstand a great deal more both physically and mentally, as has been proven repeatedly in prisoner of war camps, prisons, and concentration camps. Those who excel in the arts of meditation and/ or hypnotism can often block out pain and fatigue, displaying an uncanny and almost superhuman ability to overcome harsh circumstances. An in-depth knowledge of your Chase (see chapter 2) will provide critical clues to his mental, physical, and spiritual state.

The number and condition of the signs you come across can also be a good indication of the Chase's speed. Numerous signs that have been blatantly left behind could indicate one of two things: either the Chase is moving extremely fast, or he is luring you into a booby trap or ambush. Haphazard methods of covering signs could indicate that you are so close that the Chase doesn't have time to cover his tracks, or it could just as easily suggest that the Chase has no sense of discipline or knowledge of anti-tracking techniques or tactics. A minimal number of signs may imply that the Chase is moving slowly and methodically, covering his signs as he goes, or displaying a strict sense of discipline by leaving few signs in the first place.

Take careful note of the footprints found along the way. Shorter strides, a deeper imprint, and/or marks of dragging could be clear indicators that the Chase is carrying a heavy weight and is moving slowly. Wide, shallow imprints could likewise suggest that the Chase is carrying no load. Long strides with deep heel and toe marks as well as scattered dirt could well indicate that the Chase is running, but dragging shoe prints and a high number of top signs consisting of torn, broken, snapped, or bent foliage could be evidence of the Chase's exhaustion.

Regardless of the ease or difficulty in finding a stride, you should answer the following questions:

Is the Chase moving quickly?

Is the Chase walking? limping? carrying a heavy load?

How fast must I move to find or capture him with stealth?

Number of People

In order to know exactly what you are up against, at least in the case of a hostile pursuit, you need to have an accurate count of the number of people you are chasing. In many cases, you may not know the total number of people you are pursuing when you start out; on the other hand, the individual or group you are following may be joined by others along the way.

Determining the exact number of people who make up your Chase is again a matter of scientific—or in this case mathematical—deduction. First note the consistency in the various print patterns that you have been following. Are these individuals wearing boots, shoes, sneakers, or sandals? What kind of specific pattern do these footwear types make? Are they waffled, flat, ribbed, or cleated; do they have unique brand-specific circles, squares, or other geometric shapes? Once you have identified the type and pattern of footwear, you can concentrate on counting them.

Do the Math. Before you can mathematically calculate how many people have passed through a certain area or walked along a certain path, there are a couple of facts you must be aware of. First, you need to know that the average person does not step more than once within twenty-four inches on flat to rolling hill surfaces (once for each foot). Second, you need to account for at least one extended stride.

The calculation from here on out is relatively simple. Find a place where the group you are following has either walked across a trail or are on a trail where the composition of the soil captures the imprint of soles. Measure off twenty-four inches. Count the number of heel marks within that area, then add one for the extended stride. Example: If you counted three heel prints, add one more to account for an extended stride to equal four prints and therefore four people.

One other method is to do the math backward. For this, we must know that the average person takes a full stride within thirty-six inches (recall from chapter 4 that a full stride consists of two steps, one with each foot, and is measured between the heel of one foot to the heel of the opposite foot). In this case, we would count the prints in a thirty-six-inch area (four prints—or two full strides—per person) and divide by two. Example: If there were eight prints, divide the total by two to get a good estimate of four people.

Still one other technique is also fairly accurate in determining the correct number of people. In this case, make a note of the most prominent prints, the ones that catch the eye of the Tracker; they usually belong to the last person of the group. Measure the stride of this person, mark the stride as the left and right boundaries of the area you will be measuring (the toe of the front print and the heel of the rear print mark the top and bottom boundaries), count the number of prints within this area, and divide by two to determine the number of people.

But let's say you are in a heavily wooded area where you can't see footprints. How are you supposed to count what you can't even see? Obviously, the methods would be different here. In this instance, patience will pay off. Wait until you come across a rest or sleep site. Count the number of matted or flattened areas (consisting of live or dead vegetation or dirt) used for sitting or sleeping. Examine the trees around the site. If you see rope marks, indicating the use of hammocks, count the number of marks and divide by two (hammocks normally utilize two trees) to determine the number of sleepers—and don't forget that the same tree may be used for more than one hammock.

Kind of Food Consumed

In chapter 2 we learned quite a bit about our Chase by the types of food he consumed. By examining the food evidence left behind by our Chase, we can verify preferences, probable nationality, energy level, and even the load he is carrying. His diet will indicate whether he is killing, harvesting, or carrying his own food. Canned foods will let us know that his load, at least in terms of consumable items, is fairly heavy. Dehydrated foods will indicate a much lighter load, but they will also tell us that he needs a good supply of water to eat properly and keep himself from getting dehydrated (in other words, he may carry the water, follow streams, or zigzag from lake to pond to river).

The amount of food consumed will also provide important clues. If he is eating large quantities of food (say, over 3,000 calories per day), this might tell us that he is a very large person, is highly athletic, or is exerting a great deal of energy due to heavy loads, fast movement, or both. If he is eating minimal amounts of food (say, 1,200 calories or less), this could indicate that he is small, carrying a light load, or moving slowly due to a lack of energy.

Packages in which food has been sealed or held will also be important leads. Wrappers, labels, or the packages themselves can tell us where the food was purchased or from whom it was supplied. If we are following Colombian drug smugglers and observe weapons made exclusively in and available only from Italy, we may have stumbled across a transnational connection. If we have been chasing Burmese cross-border operatives and discover a cache containing Chinese military rations, weapons in Thailand with the markings of Vietnam, we may be up against something much larger than we anticipated, such as an international, transnational, or national connection. At that point, we need to mark the area and immediately inform higher headquarters that we may be dealing with national-level or higher operations.

Miscellaneous Items and Equipment

In order to complete the puzzle, or at least give us a much clearer picture, each item we find must be evaluated. The following is a list of articles you may run across, along with their possible meanings or indicators.

> *Bandage wrappers, gauze, or strings from a store-bought adhesive strip:* Evidence of an injury and possibly the type of injury the Chase has sustained.
>
> *Cigarette butts and chewing tobacco:* Health habits. If the Chase is a heavy smoker, it could indicate that he may run short of breath or have a hard time sustaining a fast, steady pace.
>
> *Batteries:* The use of electronic devices, such as a shaver, radio, light source, or explosives.
>
> *Toiletries such as toothpaste, foot powder, tampons, or toilet paper:* Good health habits, well-prepared, and well-equipped.

Undone traps, fishing hooks, skinned animal remains: Chase may be a survivalist.

Chopped wood: The presence of a cutting tool.

Disturbed or dug-up dirt: The presence of a digging tool, such as a shovel.

Candle wax droppings: Light source, fire source, ability to light a fuse.

Odor of white gas, ether, or lighter fluid: Light source, fire starter, camp stove, or heat-producing device.

Loose dirt: Covered wire, rope, or vines, indicating a possible booby trap; also used to cover trash, food remains, feces, or other signs.

Urine: Dark color—dehydration; bright yellow—vitamin supplements; clear or pale yellow—good hydration.

Plentiful trash and rubbish: Chase has little or no sense of discipline or is not aware someone is following him. Could also be used as a counter-tracking technique to lure you into an ambush or trap.

Weapons

Before I even approach this subject, I would like to issue a stern warning:

ANY CHASE WHO IS CARRYING A WEAPON, IDENTIFIED AS A CRIMINAL, OR CONSIDERED DANGEROUS, SHOULD NOT BE HANDLED BY TRACKERS WHO ARE NOT SUPPORTED BY THE PROPER AGENCIES. LEAVE MATTERS OF LAW ENFORCEMENT TO THOSE AUTHORIZED.

If you run across evidence of an armed criminal, soldier, or other person known to be dangerous, stop immediately and seek professional assistance. Inexperienced Trackers or single individuals who are not supported by appropriate military or law enforcement authorities should not handle these individuals. This section is intended *only* for the professional military or police tracker teams.

• • •

Knowing the types of weapons carried by your Chase will better help you when a face-to-face confrontation eventually occurs. If you are part of a team that is expected to confront an armed Chase, it is imperative that you recognize the signs to take appropriate defensive or offensive measures.

If you are not familiar with various weapon systems, identifying them will be challenging. Nevertheless, the following weapon indicators and their supporting signs should help you in their identification.

> *Knife:* Cuts on trees, shrubs, fences, rope, and other items; wood shavings. Small trees and bushes that have been cut through will indicate the presence of a large working knife, such as a machete.
>
> *Explosives:* Gunpowder; explosive materials, such as wax, rubber, kerosene, lighter fluid, or gasoline; detonating wire, timing devices, blasting caps, or batteries.
>
> *Guns* (pistol, rifle, machine gun, or submachine gun): Fired or unfired bullets; expended ammo cases (see figure 6.4), including rimless, rebated, semi-rimless, rimmed, and belted cases; the sound of gunshots; trashed magazines (see figure 6.5) or disintegrating machine-gun belt links; weapon cleaning supplies (rods, oil, cotton swabs, cotton squares, metal brushes); bipod/tripod leg impressions or rifle butt marks on the ground; viewing weapon from a distance; the sound of a bolt slamming into the chamber.

Figure 6.4 Expended ammo casings: AK-47, M-4/M-16, 9mm, 12-gauge, 45mm.

Figure 6.5 Discarded magazines: AK-47, M-4/M-16, 9mm Beretta.

Remember, never overlook or take for granted any sign. The Chase's signs will tell you a story, leaving you with an image of him. You are bound to find something that will tell you at least a little bit about your Chase, and every piece of information will eventually complete the puzzle of this pursuit. Consequently, you will become quite acquainted with the person(s) you are chasing. Keep in mind that your job is easier than your Chase's; it is very difficult for an untrained person to move through an area without leaving a sign conspicuous to the trained Tracker. The ease with which you can locate a sign will increase in proportion to the terrain's thickness and the number of Chases going in the same direction. Conversely, the sparser the terrain and the fewer the number of Chases traveling in the same direction, the greater the challenges for the Tracker.

DOCUMENTING THE EVIDENCE: THE TRACKING PATROL REPORT

You have gathered all the evidence you need, so let's go out there and pick up the Chase!

Not quite so fast. What if circumstances dictate a change in the team? Do you think the new team coming in will be able to just pick up where you left off? What if you are forced to give up the pursuit for the time being to pick it up later? Will you remember everything you have learned up to this time? What if you are involved in a mission or manhunt that is very similar to one you had a year ago? Five years ago? Will you want to reinvent the wheel and relearn your experiences? Not likely.

As the old adage says: "The job isn't finished until the paperwork is done." The same is true here. Everything you see, hear, touch, taste, and smell; everything you pick up; every assumption you make; every piece to the puzzle must be carefully recorded as you go along. And it must be documented in such a manner that another team can read it and pick up the trail where you left off. It could also help you recall the details of another pursuit, saving yourself hours, maybe days of time, relearning the lessons of a previous mission, and it could save you a great deal of embarrassment by helping you to avoid mistakes that were made the first time. Perhaps a more experienced Tracker, or one with a different background, may recognize a sign that you did not or may more accurately interpret a sign you recorded.

Difficult or not, the information must be gathered, dissected, and presented in a Tracking Patrol Report.

Overview

Upon return from a search area or area of operation, a Tracker should be able to prepare and present an official report of what transpired during the conduct of the search. This information must be accurate, timely, and gathered systematically and continuously for ongoing Tracker teams and those personnel with a need to know in order to confirm, deny, or bring to light additional information about the Chase. Throughout history, many searches and missions have been distinguishably successful due to the reports delivered by Trackers.

This report must be written and/or presented verbally (perhaps enhanced with still pictures, videotape, and the like), but a written document is preferable if time allows. Recording detailed descriptions of the evidence in a notebook, with an illustration of the incident, will help the Tracker articulate the incident in the Tracking Patrol Report. Either way, the report must be based on undeniable facts and hard evidence to maintain the reliability of the data.

131

Note that I intentionally used the word "fact," which is "an actual occurrence: an event: a piece of information presented as having an objective reality."[27] The Tracking Patrol Report is based on facts. Information gathered and recorded as exhibits must be based on undeniable, hard evidence, which allows you to *interpret* what is seen or sensed, thus permitting you to dissect the facts using *deductive reasoning* in a logical manner (based on your experience in tracking or in life). Incident Report is a stand-alone report that can be added to the Tracking Patrol Report. The Tracking Patrol Report is basically composed of a series of Incident Reports (see appendix C "Incident Report").

The Tracking Patrol Report is the means by which you can document and establish a strong hypothesis firmly based on data that will answer the questions of what, when, where, why, and how the signs were formed, as well as who made them. The Tracking Patrol Report should also include an assumption, which is a conclusive statement that in its entirety conveys the facts and then comes to a conclusion of the Chase's task or anticipated intention. Based on these facts and the Tracker's hypothesis, the Tracker should be able to make a logical, reasonable assumption, and then finally present in the Tracking Patrol Report a conclusive recommendation about the Chase in order to brief ongoing tracker teams and other personnel.

You must seek, gather, record, and preserve the soundness of your evidence in order to learn and share as much as possible about your Chase. This process will ultimately validate your delivered oral or written Tracking Patrol Report and, in the process, reward you with the recognition as a credible Tracker.

Remember, a sign, like a still picture, is merely a snapshot of a one-time occurrence. An incident is a collection of signs that describe a scene, an area where a person was last seen walking, standing, or camping; the place from which a person was abducted; or the site where a firefight or ambush occurred. But taken together, a collection of incidents begin to shape themselves into a story, much like the individual frames of an 8mm film combine into scenes to make a full-length movie.

Signs gathered in such a manner that they are destroyed in the process are, in the end, no evidence at all. If homicide detectives contaminate blood evidence or cover the suspect's fingerprints with their own,

27 *Webster's Ninth Collegiate Dictionary,* s.v. "fact."

the evidence gathered is worthless and cannot be admitted in a criminal trial. Similarly, although not perhaps to the extent of a criminal case, signs gathered in the process of a pursuit cannot be further examined for clues if they have been damaged or destroyed. The bottom line is, all evidence must be sought, found, gathered, preserved, and recorded in such a manner that maintains its integrity throughout the entire process.

Searching

In order for the collected evidence to be accurate and complete, a systematic approach must be taken. It must be comprehensive, thorough, and efficient, and answer as many of the basic interrogatories (*who, what, when, where, why,* and *how*) as possible. Well-defined search patterns conducted by the lead Tracker will normally accomplish this.

There are three types of patterns I have found most effective either as a sole Tracker or as a member of a team within the incident area:

Grid Method. This method divides up the search area by walking a parallel, evenly measured, crisscrossing pattern (see figure 6.6). Start in one corner and move systematically up the length of the incident area, then cut back in a parallel path until you reach the near end next to your starting point, and once again turn and head in the original direction until the entire area has been searched. After that, make a ninety-degree turn and repeat the pattern until you have combed through the entire incident area. If on a team, the team members secure the perimeter of the incident, while the Tracker and coverman (on a hostile chase) move forward to carefully search until the entire area has been covered.

Coil Method. The uncoiling/coiling method is used most often when a Tracker is alone, but can be adapted to accommodate a team. In this pattern, the Tracker moves to and starts at the center of the incident area, being mindful of booby traps and using appropriate caution so as not to disturb any prospective signs. He then moves in a circular, uncoiling manner, creating a pattern very similar to that of a coiled rope rug or stovetop heating element (see figure 6.7). The key is to maintain, ideally, a distance of about three yards or meters from the previous ring—depending, of course, on the terrain, foliage, and visibility—until the perimeter of the

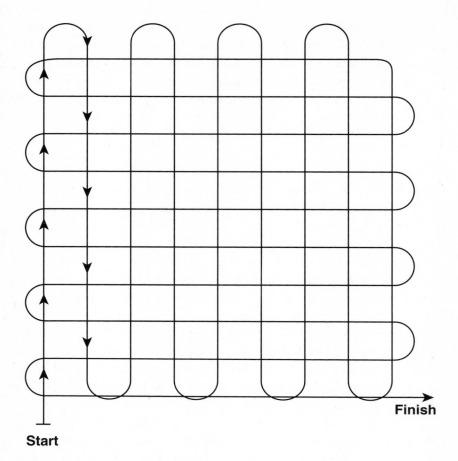

Finish

Start

Figure 6.6 Grid method.

incident area has been reached. If he is not satisfied with the conduct or results of the search, the Tracker should turn around and recoil his pattern.

Additionally, if there is great concern that starting in the center of the incident area could damage or destroy valid signs, the reverse of this method can also be used. In this instance, the Tracker or team starts at the perimeter of the incident area with a wide, sweeping circle that then coils inward in ever-tighter rings until the center has been reached.

Fan Method. This method lays out a pattern that resembles a fan. The Tracker starts from the center point and turns directly to the right or left.

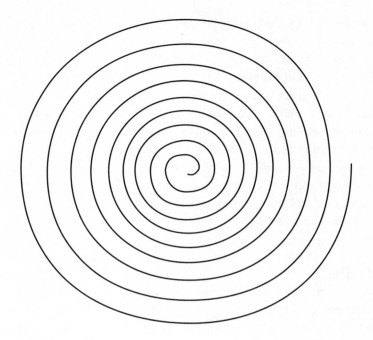

Figure 6.7 Coil method.

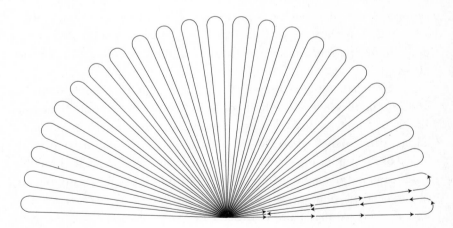

Figure 6.8 Fan method.

He proceeds outward from there, makes a looping U-turn inward, and returns to the center point. The next loop lays down a pattern to the interior side of and nearly parallel to the first, and so on, until the fan is complete (see figure 6.8).

In a nonhostile chase, the area should be cordoned off while the Tracker and/or main investigator conduct the search. In a hostile chase, a perimeter security must be emplaced before the Tracker and coverman move forward to conduct the search.

Never make the mistake of carelessly approaching the initial, obvious sign. Approaching the obvious can destroy evidence between you and the observed sign. Or, worse yet, it could be a lure, intended to draw you into a booby trap or ambush.

Recording

As each Tracker comes across a notable sign, or one not previously seen, he or she must make a record of it with detailed descriptions. Using common words that can easily be understood by all team members and others likely to read the report, document every possible detail about the sign or incident. List the indicators that led up to the discovery. Record the number, texture, and approximate size and shape of the sign; describe the condition it was in when it was found, as well as its features, construction, and color(s). Make a note of the date, time, location (using appropriate pinpoint map coordinates), and weather conditions at the time of the discovery.

I reminded you in chapter 2 that a picture paints a thousand words. The same applies here. No matter how detailed your description, there will always be room for inaccuracies, misunderstandings, or distorted mental pictures. Following your written description, therefore, make a visual image of the sign using whatever means are available. If you have brought a still camera (preferably a 35mm SLR, Polaroid, or high density digital camera), take a photograph; if you have the luxury of carrying a video camera or camcorder, make a videotape that views the sign from all angles and includes the surrounding area. If you merely have a piece of paper and a writing instrument, draw an illustration in as much detail as your artistic abilities will allow.

The best writing instrument to use is a simple wooden lead pencil. Why? (1) It doesn't smear; (2) it's easy to sharpen with a knife; (3) broken in two, it provides two pencils; (4) it is the least expensive of all potential writing instruments.

Likewise, I have found that the digital camera/camcorder is tops when it comes to photographic equipment. It takes both still pictures and video; it is compact, versatile (some are IR/thermal capable), and highly portable; it stores a high volume of pictures on a tiny disk. The team can immediately see or repeatedly review the pictures taken, without waiting for lengthy, costly film development. In the long run, it is by far the most cost-effective.

Taking a photo is great and convenient if you do not have the time to sketch what you are seeing and note what you are smelling and experiencing. But sketching the particular sign, track, or incident site is better because you are actually taking a more personal approach. You're sensing and placing this sign more firmly in your memory. You do not have to be a Picasso, as long as you know what you are drawing and you can interpret it. It would be great to be able to draw a sketch so that all involved can see what you are seeing, but what is more important is that you are embedding the information in your memory much better than you would just by taking a quick photo. In my classes I have the students take the photo *and* draw a sketch to see the difference. Hand to paper to memory works better than just photo to memory. Even if you do not have the time on-site, make a sketch of the photo when you do have time or have gone back to you base of operation (office or campsite). This review will also aid your recall.

Collecting

If the sign you have found is transportable, such as communications wire, by all means accumulate and preserve it. Now obviously, a boot print on the ground, a scratch on a rock, or a cut on a tree is not a sign you can collect. Even though these can be plastered, time constraints will not permit it under hostile conditions nor would it be practical to do so. With these signs, you will just have to be satisfied with written descriptions, sketches, and photographs.

So how do you pick up and store items that could easily become contaminated or destroyed? Very simply, you must have the appropriate tools. This includes common items that you can purchase from nearly any store that carries pharmacy and/or camping supplies. Some of the most common items are tweezers; gloves (surgical, tight-fitting, or rubber gloves in newer first-aid kits, or other lightweight cloth or leather gloves); a small retractable measuring tape; a magnifying glass; ziplock bags, Tupperware-like containers, film canisters, pill bottles, or other containers with tight-fitting lids.

Within reason, items should not be picked up with the bare hand. Poisons, chemical or biological agents, or acidic residues remaining on the item could burn your skin, damage your eyes or the thin membranes in your nose, throat, or lungs, absorb into your bloodstream, or gain access to sensitive body cavities such as your eyes, ears, nose, open wounds, and private areas. Conversely, oil from your hands could discolor certain metals, cause delicate flowers to wilt, or contaminate sterile fields. Even the powder from certain types of rubber gloves could damage some articles.

The rule here is, cover your hands and use your judgment on the best means to collect the object. For very small items, tweezers may be the most suitable collection method; for others, fingers, vise-grips, or small garden shovels may prove the most appropriate.

Closely examine the item with a magnifying glass, making note of any serial numbers, codes, or other marks etched, drawn, painted, stamped, or stenciled onto it. Measure it with a measuring tape or micrometer. Then place it carefully into a suitable bag or container, seal it, and pack it in a manner that will preclude damage.

Formatting

Just as you have systematically found and gathered your evidence, you must also systematically record it. You may use any format you choose, as long as it covers all the points discussed in this chapter. For many years, I have used a Tracking Patrol Report format that serves just such a purpose. A sample of this report, based on our Korean infiltrator scenario, follows this chapter. A blank version of this report is contained in appendix D.

Not only does this report capture the six interrogatories and a detailed description of each item found, it also contains summary sections that add to and make conclusions about what has been gathered.

Interpretation. All of the facts gathered along the way must be dissected, interpreted, and combined with assumptions in order to come up with realistic deductions about the conduct of the Chase. In order to conduct future planning or refine existing plans, you must come up with a hypothesis regarding your Chase's expected actions, so you can better anticipate, thwart, or defend yourself against them.

Assumptions. I said earlier that all evidence must be based on fact. That is not to say you cannot make assumptions—conclusive statements that are based on fact but not specifically seen or experienced. Assumptions are necessary to bridge the gap between two known pieces of information in order to form a well-grounded conclusion about your Chase's mission and/or anticipated movements.

Recommendation. Finally, your report should conclude with recommendations for your possible courses of action (in ongoing operations), lessons learned from recently completed missions, and/or suggestions for future operations.

Completed properly, your Tracking Patrol Report should be able to be picked up, read, and understood by any other Tracker who knows your language and is at least somewhat familiar with the territory you are describing. Standardization of the Tracking Patrol Reports, which may be modified for your department or agency, will simplify the transition or hand-over procedures from one agency to another across the board. A good test of this might be to give your report to a Tracker from another professional group. Soldiers can give their reports to Trackers from the Central Intelligence Agency (CIA); a search and rescue team can hand theirs to law enforcement officers; forest rangers can turn theirs over to a search and rescue team; and a group of US Army Rangers can present theirs to a Tracker team from another branch of service to ensure completeness, simplicity, and clarity for all who may follow.

Okay. We know how to interpret signs, preserve the incident area, and gather evidence. We know how to complete the paperwork. Now what?

"Gentlemen! Gather up some men and deputize them. We are going to round up the posse!"

TRACKING PATROL REPORT

OPERATION: CHASE

PATROL DESIGNATION: TT JERSEY 266

AREA OF OPERATION :   EASTERN 33 TO 36   NORTHERN 83 TO 86

MAP REFERENCES: SERIES FRST MISC 54, SCALE 1:25,000
                                         SHEET 21–52, EDITION 9

PATROL COMPOSITION:

NAME	POSITION
CW3 GARY JORDAN	DETACHMENT COMMANDER
MSG MALUPA TUMERA (SAMOA)	TEAM LEADER
SFC FRANCISCO BADILLO (FRANK)	WEAPONS SERGEANT, TRACKER
SFC PAUL O'CONNOR	TEAM MEDIC, SECONDARY TRACKER, AND COVERMAN
SFC ROBERT ROWE	RADIO OPERATOR
MAJOR KIM CHONG HEE	KOREAN ADVISOR

1. MISSION: TO SEEK, LOCATE, IDENTIFY, AND PURSUE SIGNS IN ORDER TO CAPTURE
NORTH KOREAN INFILTRATORS.

2. TIMINGS: A. INFIL: 30 06:30 MAR 02
                    B. EXFIL: 01 15:00 APRIL 02

3. INFIL POINT: LP 230GR 334863   METHOD: FOOT

4. EXFIL POINT: LP 230GR 335831   METHOD: HELICOPTER

5. GROUND: KUM-GANG (RIVER) BEING THE MAIN WATER FEATURE RUNNING FROM
NORTH TO SOUTH, THE AREA HAS A LONG RANGE OF MOUNTAINS THAT CRISSCROSS
WITH NUMEROUS HILLS AND RIDGES PROLIFERATING. MANY RIDGES, WITH STEEP SIDES,
RISE TO OVER 4000 FEET. IN SOME OF THESE HIGH ALTITUDES, THERE ARE MANY SMALL
PATCHES OF FARMLAND AND AREAS FOR GRAZING CATTLE. TRACKS EXIST ON THE MAIN
RIDGES AND ARE USED BY LOCALS WHEN PICKING MUSHROOMS AND OCCASIONALLY
WHEN VISITING THEIR SACRED HAPPY MOUNDS (BURIAL SITES) OR MOVING CATTLE FROM
ONE GRAZING AREA TO ANOTHER. STREAMS ARE PLENTIFUL DURING THE RAINY SEASON,
AND THEY MAINLY RUN EAST TO WEST, JOINING THE KUM-GANG (RIVER). (SEE ANNEX A)

DAY ONE

FROM START POINT 280 WE TRAVELED EAST PARALLELING THE NONSAN-CHON (RIVER)
FOR A DISTANCE OF 900 METERS TO GRID 342861. AT THIS LOCATION WE PICKED UP THE
ENEMY SIGN, A BOOT PRINT (SEE INCIDENT ONE, EXHIBIT ONE; AND ANNEX B). FROM
THIS PLACE, WE TRAVELED EAST, CROSSING THE NONSAN-CHON (RIVER), ON A BEARING
OF 1700mls, FOR A DISTANCE OF 900 METERS, WHERE WE LOCATED A POSSIBLE MEAL
HALT AT GRID 351859 (SEE INCIDENT TWO, EXHIBIT TWO, AND ANNEX C). FROM HERE WE
MOVED AN ADDITIONAL 600 METERS ON A BEARING OF 1700mls, AND LAID UP FOR THE
NIGHT, AT GRID 355859.

DAY TWO

AT A BEARING OF 1100mls, WE CONTINUED UP TO A KNOLL FOR 100 METERS, AND AT GRID 357859 WE CHANGED DIRECTION TO A BEARING OF 4410mls. AT THAT POINT WE FOLLOWED THE RIDGELINE FOR A DISTANCE OF 900 METERS, WHERE WE DROPPED DOWN OFF THE RIDGELINE ON A BEARING OF 4000mls FOR 280 METERS. WE CROSSED THE YONG CHIANG (STREAM) AT GRID 346854. THERE WE FOUND A HARBOR SITE (SLEEP SITE/MEAL HALT), EVIDENCE OF SOME KIND OF COPPER ELECTRICAL WIRE, USED MOST APPARENTLY FOR COMMUNICATION EQUIPMENT, AND A BUTT IMPRINT OF AN AKM WEAPON (SEE INCIDENT THREE, EXHIBITS THREE AND FOUR; AND ANNEX D). AT THAT MOMENT WE CHANGED DIRECTION TO A BEARING OF 2410mls, FOR A DISTANCE OF 220 METERS TO A KNOLL WHERE A HAPPY MOUND WAS SITTING AT GRID 347853. THEREAFTER, WE TRAVELED DOWN THE RIDGELINE TO THE SOUTHEAST AT A BEARING OF 2120mls FOR 700 METERS, NOTING A FEW POINTERS AT WAIST AND SHOULDER HEIGHT. WE CROSSED THE BAGDOE CHON (RIVER) OVER A LARGE DEADFALL AND LOCATED A POSSIBLE SHORT HALT AT GRID 349847 (SEE INCIDENT FOUR AND ANNEX E). FROM HERE WE TRAVELED ON A BEARING OF 2800mls, FOR A DISTANCE OF 100 METERS. WE THEN CHANGED DIRECTIONS TO A BEARING OF 3880mls, 250 METERS TO A HILL AT GRID 348845. THEREUPON, WE TRAVELED ON A BEARING OF 2390mls FOR A DISTANCE OF 500 METERS WHERE WE LAID UP FOR THE NIGHT AT GRID 351842.

DAY THREE

ON A BEARING OF 3980mls FOR 400 METERS WE WENT DOWN A FINGER THEN CROSSED THE HUN CHIANG (STREAM) CONTINUING ON THE SAME AZIMUTH FOR AN ADDITIONAL 500 METERS, WHERE WE NOTICED FRESH POINTERS, INDICATING DOWNWARD MOBILITY. WE CROSSED THE YEONG CHIANG (STREAM) AND CONTINUED ON THE SAME AZIMUTH FOR 100 METERS, THEN CHANGED DIRECTIONS. ON A BEARING OF 2340mls WE SEARCHED AROUND A KNOLL AT GRID 34698346. THROUGHOUT THIS PURSUIT, SIGNS WERE PRETTY MUCH OBSCURED, UNTIL WE MOVED AN ADDITIONAL 100 METERS. AT GRID 34688339 WE LOCATED A DEFINITE HARBOR SITE (SEE INCIDENT FIVE, EXHIBIT FIVE, AND ANNEX F). FROM THIS POINT WE MOVED, ON A BEARING OF 4800mls, IN A CAREFUL HURRY, KNOWING THAT IMMINENT CONTACT WAS AT HAND, FOR FRESH POINTERS AT WAIST LEVEL WERE NOTED WHILE GOING DOWNHILL. FRESH SHOE PRINTS WERE BY THE YEONG CHIANG (STREAM), THE SAME PRINT FOUND IN INCIDENT ONE (SEE EXHIBIT ONE). MOVING IN A WESTERLY DIRECTION WE FOLLOWED THE CHASE, PARALLELING SOUTH OF THE YEONG CHIANG (STREAM), UNTIL WE MADE CONTACT. AT GRID 337833 A FIREFIGHT TOOK PLACE AT 13:45. WITHIN THIS LOCATION WE CONSOLIDATED AND REORGANIZED. AT 14:10 WE LINKED UP WITH LOCAL MILITARY AND BOTH US AND SOUTH KOREAN GOVERNMENT AGENCIES, AT WHICH TIME WE RELINQUISHED COMMAND AND CONTROL TO THEM. WE THEN MOVED ON A BEARING OF 3810mls FOR A DISTANCE OF 210 METERS TO OUR EXFILTRATION SITE, WHERE AT 15:00 WE WERE EXTRACTED.

* THE CONSTANT OFF AND ON OF THE DRIZZLING SOUND OF RAIN COVERED OUR MOVEMENT FOR NOISE. THE RAIN ALLOWED FOR SIGNS TO BE MADE AND LEFT WITH EASE. YET, THE RAIN WAS NOT STRONG ENOUGH TO WASH AWAY THE SIGNS LEFT IN FRONT OF US BY THE CHASE. THE WEATHER CONDITION AIDED US A GREAT DEAL IN THE CAPTURING OF OUR CHASE.

6. INTERPRETATION AND DEDUCTION (INTER-DEDUCTION)

INCIDENT	DAY	FACTS	INTER-DEDUCTION
01	ONE	AT GRID 342861 ALONG THE NONSAN-CHON, A TIRE-PATTERN SHOE PRINT WAS FOUND (SEE EXHIBIT ONE AND ANNEX B). THE SOILS COMPOSITION ALSO EXPOSED A VERY DEEP IMPRINT. THIS WAS A GOOD SITE FOR A WATER RESUPPLY.	THE DISTINCT PATTERN WITH MODERATE WEAR EDGE OF THE PATTERN INDICATES THAT THE BOOT WAS WELL BROKEN IN, AS IF A SEASONED VETERAN WOULD HAVE TO NEGOTIATE THIS RUGGED TERRAIN. THE DEEP PRINT INDICATES THAT THEY ARE CARRYING HEAVY EQUIPMENT. IF THIS WAS A WATER RESUPPLY SITE, THEN WATER CONTAINERS AND SOME SOURCE OF WATER PURIFICA-TION ARE AVAILABLE.
02	ONE	WE FOUND FOUR AREAS OF FLATTENED GRASS AT GRID 351859. CRUMBS OF CRACKERS AND VERY SMALL RICE GRAINS WERE ALSO DISCOVERED. THERE WERE THREE SMALL BURNT AREAS ON THE GROUND (SEE EXHIBIT TWO AND ANNEX C).	DUE TO THE PATTERN OF THE AREAS OF FLATTENING, IT WOULD APPEAR THAT FOUR PEOPLE SAT IN ALL-AROUND SECURITY. THE WAY THE GROUND WAS BURNT INDICATED THAT THE CHASE HAD SOME HEAT SOURCE FOR COOKING. BREAKING AWAY FROM THEIR PATH, SITTING IN A DEFENSIVE POSTURE, AND LEAVING MINIMAL AMOUNTS OF SIGNS INDICATE THEY WERE MOTIVATED, COMMITTED PROFESSIONALS WITH A PURPOSE. THE CRACKERS AND THE RICE INDICATE THEY HAVE RATIONS.
03	TWO	AT GRID 346854 WE FOUND SHAVEN AND TUBULAR RESIDUE OF COLOR-CODED BLACK-AND-WHITE RUBBER (SEE EXHIBIT THREE AND ANNEX D). WE ALSO FOUND THREE AREAS OF FLATTENED GRASS, THREE BURNT AREAS, AND A WELL-DEPICTED IMPRINT OF THE BUTT OF AN AK-47 (SEE EXHIBIT FOUR AND ANNEX D).	THE PRECISE SURGICAL CUTS AROUND THE COLOR-CODED RUBBER INDICATE USE OF A PROFESSIONAL ELECTRICAL CUTTING TOOL, FOR NO METALLIC RESIDUE WAS NOTED. THE TUBULAR RESIDUE SURELY SUGGESTS THE USE OF WIRE. THE USE OF WIRE OF THIS DIMENSION INDICATES IMPROVISED OR MANUFACTURED EXPLOSIVES OR COMMUNICATIONS EQUIPMENT AT THEIR DISPOSAL. DUE TO THE PATTERN OF THE AREAS OF FLATTENING, THIS WAS A SLEEP SITE. APPARENTLY, THREE

INCIDENT	DAY	FACTS	INTER-DEDUCTION
(03 cont.)			PEOPLE SLEPT WHILE ONE STOOD GUARD. THE IMPRINT OF THE AK-47 SUGGESTS THAT THEY POSSESS AUTOMATIC WEAPONS. THE BURNT AREAS FURTHER CONFIRM A HEAT SOURCE FOR COOKING.
04	TWO	AT GRID 349847 WE FOUND FOUR DISTURBANCES THAT HAD A SOMEWHAT FLATTENED APPEARANCE, WITH A POSSIBLE FIFTH (SEE ANNEX E).	THE DISCOVERY OF MINIMAL SIGNS IS AN INDICATION OF A DEFENSIVE POSTURE. THE SIGNS WERE NOT TOO EMBEDDED, AS IF IT WERE A SHORT SECURITY HALT OR NAVIGATION CHECK.
05	THREE	AT GRID 346834 WE FOUND FOUR AREAS OF FLATTENING AND A POSSIBLE FIFTH. THERE WAS ONE BURNT AREA WITH SOME SMALL AMOUNTS OF COOKED WHITE RICE AND GARLIC SKIN (SEE EXHIBIT FIVE AND ANNEX F). THERE WERE ROPE MARKS ON TREES.	THESE FOUR DISTINCTIVE AREAS OF FLATTENING LED US TO BELIEVE THAT THERE ARE FOUR PEOPLE IN THIS PATROL AND/OR A POSSIBLE FIFTH. THE BURNT GROUND AND FOOD WITHIN THE 1/2 METER AREA INDICATE ONE PERSON MAY HAVE BEEN COOKING FOR THE ENTIRE PATROL. THE PATTERN OF FLATTENING INDICATES AN ALL-AROUND DEFENSE. THE USE OF GARLIC AND RICE MAY INDICATE THAT THE ENEMY IS POSSIBLY OF ASIAN ORIGIN, MOST LIKELY OF KOREAN DESCENT. THEN AGAIN THE CHASE MAY BE PROFESSIONALS FROM ANOTHER COUNTRY, EATING NATIVE FOOD IN ORDER TO BLEND IN WITH THE LOCALS. THE EXCESSIVE SIGNS INDICATE THAT THE CHASE WAS SURELY IN A RUSH TO LEAVE, DUE TO THE TEAM'S CLOSE PROXIMITY. THE ROPE MARKS ON THE TREES INDICATE THEY WERE USING HAMMOCKS.

7. ASSUMPTIONS:

THE INFILTRATORS WERE USING GOOD TACTICS AND LEAVING FEW SIGNS UNTIL WE CLOSED IN AND BECAME AN IMMINENT THREAT, AT GRID 346834. THEY WERE USING ROUTES THAT WERE FREQUENTED BY LOCALS, INDICATING THAT EITHER THEY DID NOT CONSIDER THE LOCALS A THREAT, OR THE LOCALS WERE SUPPORTING THEM, OR THEY KNEW AT WHAT TIME TO EXPOSE THEMSELVES WITHOUT COMPROMISE. THIS HELPED COVER THEIR SIGNS, DUE TO THE CONTAMINATION FROM THE LOCALS' TRACKS. THE LACK OF HARBOR SITES REINFORCED THE FACT THAT THEY WERE VERY PROFESSIONAL USING DECEPTIVE TACTICS. THE FACT THAT THEY COOKED RICE, HAD GARLIC, AND LEFT A DEEP TIRE-PATTERN IMPRINT OF A BOOT INDICATES THEY HAD LOAD-CARRYING EQUIPMENT, WATER CONTAINERS, A SOURCE OF WATER PURIFICATION, A HEAT SOURCE, AND COOKING UTENSILS. THE IMPRINT OF THE BUTT OF THE AKM 47 WAS FOUND. THIS ALLOWED FOR THE ASSUMPTION THAT THEY WERE CARRYING AUTOMATIC WEAPONS WITH NUMEROUS MAGAZINES LOADED WITH 30 ROUNDS EACH OF 7.62 ROUNDS. THE FOLLOWING OF RIDGELINES AND TRAVELING CROSS-COUNTRY INDICATE MAP READING EQUIPMENT. BASED ON THE SEIZED EXPLOSIVES AND BIOCHEMICALS, AS WELL AS THEIR DIRECTION OF MOVEMENT, THE CHASE LED US TO BELIEVE THAT THEY WERE GOING TO RELEASE THE BIOCHEMICALS IN THE ANDONG CHOSUJI (WATER RESERVOIR).

8. INFORMATION GAINED:

A. STRENGTH: 4–5

B. WEAPONS: 4 AKM 7.62mm X 39mm RIFLES; ONE PISTOL 7.62 TYPE 64 WITH SILENCER

C. AMMUNITION/DEMO: 7.62mm X 39mm AMMO; 7.62mm X SR17mm; ELECTRONIC EXPLOSIVE DEVICE

D. LOAD/EQUIPMENT: AMMUNITION POUCHES AND WEAPONS CLEANING KIT. BACKPACK, POSSIBLE RADIO SIGNAL EQUIPMENT, AND MEDICAL KIT. MAP READING AND LAND NAVIGATIONAL AIDS. COOKING EQUIPMENT AND WATER CONTAINERS.

E. AGE: START: 3–4 HRS.

FINISH: 10 MINUTES–0

F. MORALE: VERY HIGH

9. CONFIRMATION:

I.   CAPTURED WAS ONE NORTH KOREAN INFILTRATOR.
II.   K.I.A. WERE TWO NORTH KOREAN INFILTRATORS.
III. RESCUED WAS A SOUTH KOREAN CIVILIAN.
IV.   SEIZED WAS:

   a. THREE ALUMINUM ALLOYED CYLINDERS, APPROXIMATELY TWO FEET LONG AND FIVE INCHES IN DIAMETER, WITH A TIMED ELECTRONIC EXPLOSIVE DEVICE STAMPED IN KOREAN AND TRANSLATED AS "CHEMICAL PRODUCT OF KANGGYE AND SAKCHU FACTORIES."

   b. THE EXPLOSIVES HAD A DUAL-INITIATING SYSTEM:

      1. REMOTE SIGNALING.

      2. TIME.

c. THREE CLAYMORES WITH ACCESSORIES. IN THE CLAYMORE BAGS THERE WERE TWO DUAL PRIMED PRECUT TIME FUSES.

    1. 30-SEC. DELAY TIME FUSE.

    2. ONE-MINUTE DELAY TIME FUSE.

    3. ONE TWO-MINUTE DELAY TIME FUSE

d. FOUR AKMs 7.62mm x 39mm TYPE 68 WITH CHINESE FOLDING HORSESHOE DESIGN STOCKS THAT HAVE PERFORATED RAILS, JOINED AT THE STOCK (AUTOMATIC ASSAULT RIFLES). TWO 7.62mm x SR17mm TYPE 64 PISTOLS WITH SILENCERS. THIS PISTOL IS LIKE THE BROWNING MODEL 1900.

    1. FORTY 30-ROUND MAGAZINES, 300 ROUNDS OF 7.62mm x 39mm WERE RETRIEVED. (EVERY THIRD ROUND WAS A TRACER).

    2. SIXTEEN 10-ROUND MAGAZINES, 150 ROUNDS OF 7.62mm x SR17mm WERE RETRIEVED.

e. ONE MEDICAL BAG WITH IVs, SUTURE KIT, VARIOUS GAUZES AND SIZES, PRESSURE BANDAGES, TAPE, ETC. EACH MEMBER HAD CYANIDE CAPSULES AND PRESSURE BANDAGE.

f. THREE BACKPACKS, ONE GPS, FIVE COMPASSES, TWO MAPS OF OUR AREA OF OPERATION, TWO MONOCULAR NIGHT VISION DEVICES, TWO BINOCULARS.

g. ONE SET OF COOKING UTENSILS. SOME RICE WAS PRE-COOKED. SOME MEALS WERE LIKE READY-TO-EAT MEALS, SIMILAR TO US RATIONS. THREE SMALL SINGLE-BURNER STOVES.

10. RECOMMENDATIONS:

a. DURING THE AREA SEARCH, THE SOLDIERS IN KEY POSITIONS NORTH OF US SHOULD HAVE MOVED SOUTH, EXCEPT THE ONES AT CRITICAL TARGET AREAS, CONSIDERING WE WERE ON A POSITIVE PATH OF THE CHASE.

b. A TWELVE-MAN COALITION TEAM SHOULD HAVE BEEN TRAILING US NO CLOSER THAN 500 METERS, CONSIDERING THE TERRAIN, FOR ON-THE-GROUND BACKUP, IN THE EVENT WE WERE OVERTAKEN BY THE INFILTRATORS.

c. DURING FUTURE TRAINING EVENTS, ALL PARTIES SHOULD REHEARSE LINK UP AND COMMAND/CONTROL PROCEDURES FOR JOINT COALITION TYPES OF OPERATION, IN ORDER TO PREVENT FRIENDLY FIRE.

ROUTE
MAP OVERLAY OF A.O.: Eastern 33 to 36
Northern 83 to 86

ANNEX: A
TO: TRACKER REP.
DATED: 02 APR 02

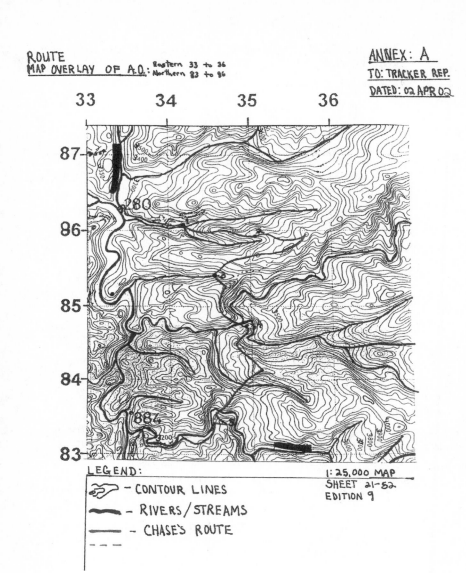

33   34   35   36

87-
86-
85-
84-
83-

280

884

LEGEND:

- CONTOUR LINES
- RIVERS/STREAMS
- CHASE'S ROUTE

1:25,000 MAP
SHEET 21-52
EDITION 9

INCIDENT-1

GRD: 342861

DTG: 300830 HRS MAR 02

N

ANNEX B

TO: TRACKER REP.

DATED: 02 APR 02

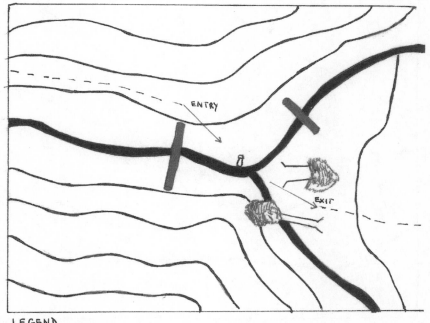

ENTRY

EXIT

LEGEND

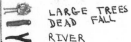

- - - - ROUTE TAKEN

CONTOUR LINE

ENTRY/EXIT

BOOT PRINT

LARGE TREES

DEAD FALL

RIVER

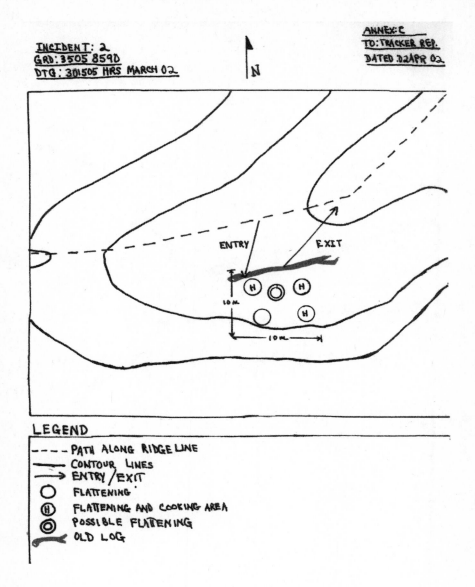

ENTRY

EXIT

10 M.

10 M.

LEGEND

- - - - PATH ALONG RIDGE LINE

———— CONTOUR LINES

———→ ENTRY / EXIT

○ FLATTENING

Ⓗ FLATTENING AND COOKING AREA

◎ POSSIBLE FLATTENING

〰 OLD LOG

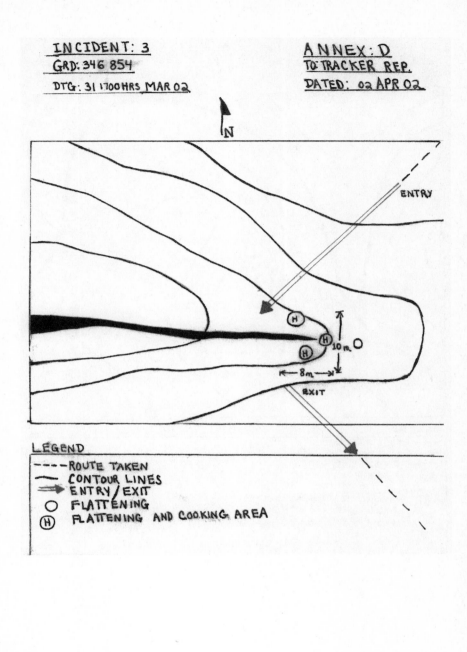

INCIDENT: 3
GRD: 346 854
DTG: 31 1700 HRS MAR 02

ANNEX: D
TO: TRACKER REP.
DATED: 02 APR 02

N

ENTRY

10 m

8m

EXIT

LEGEND
---- ROUTE TAKEN
CONTOUR LINES
ENTRY/EXIT
○ FLATTENING
Ⓗ FLATTENING AND COOKING AREA

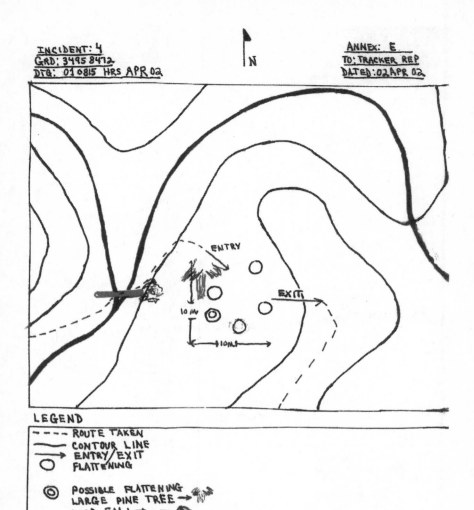

INCIDENT: 4
GRID: 3495 8472
DTG: 01 0815 HRS APR 02

N

ANNEX: E
TO: TRACKER REP
DATED: 02 APR 02

ENTRY

EXIT

10 M

10 M

LEGEND

- - - - ROUTE TAKEN
‾‾‾‾‾ CONTOUR LINE
——→ ENTRY/EXIT
◯ FLATTENING

◎ POSSIBLE FLATTENING
LARGE PINE TREE →
DEAD FALL →

INCIDENT: 5
GRD: 3468 8339
DTG: 011145 APR 02

ANNEX: F
TO: TRACKER REP
DATED: 02 APR 02

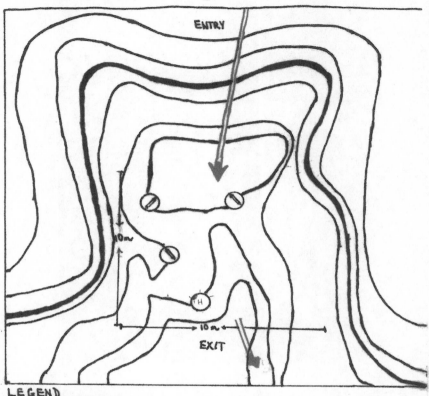

N

ENTRY

10m

10m

EXIT

LEGEND

→ ENTRY/EXIT

〜〜 CONTOUR LINE

〜〜 STREAM

⊘ FLATTENING/HAMMOCK

Ⓗ FLATTENING

INCIDENT   ONE
DAY   ONE
EXHIBIT   ONE
DESCRIPTION:
    Composition of the soil exposed a distinct,
deep tire like foot wear pattern.
    1. Quarter of an inch deep.
    2. Twelth inches long.
    3. Five inches wide, at the ball.
    4. four inches wide, at the heal.

INCIDENT   TWO
DAY   ONE
EXHIBIT   TWO

DESCRIPTION:
     Uncooked, small grain, white
     rice and cracker crumbs.

INCIDENT   THREE
DAY   TWO
EXHIBIT   FOUR

DESCRIPTION:
        APPEARS TO BE THE BUTT OF
    A CHINESE FOLDING STOCK AKM
    7.62 mm X 39mm TYPE 68

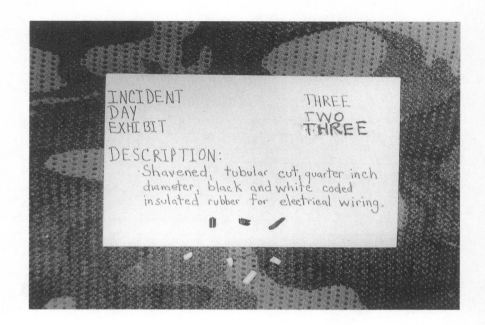

INCIDENT   THREE
DAY   TWO
EXHIBIT   THREE

DESCRIPTION:
    Shavened, tubular cut, quarter inch
    diameter, black and white coded
    insulated rubber for electrical wiring.

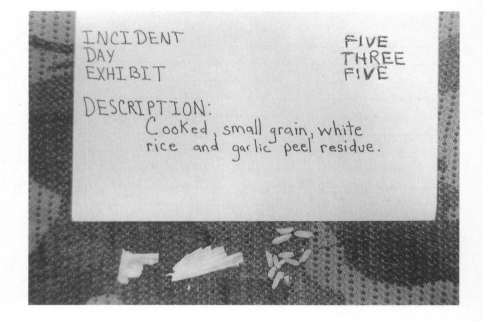

INCIDENT   FIVE
DAY   THREE
EXHIBIT   FIVE

DESCRIPTION:
    Cooked, small grain, white
    rice and garlic peel residue.

CHAPTER 7

Round Up the Posse

*We live in an age fit for heroes. No time has ever
offered such perils or such prizes. What is needed
is people who will keep their heads in an emergency
no matter what the field.*

—VINCE LOMBARDI

*This means building "Team Spirit": this means
common goals, complementary skills and abilities,
and mutual accountability.*

—VINCE LOMBARDI JR.

In the rough and semicivilized days of the Old West, the courageous sheriff would gather together the townspeople, deputize willing volunteers, and round up his posse to go after the hapless and, they hoped, overwhelmed outlaw. There were many failures yet many lessons learned during the actual pursuits of the 1800s.

Although some were highly organized, the stereotypical posse from the Old West was haphazard at best. The sheriff had an idea of which people he would end up with on each pursuit, but even so, he couldn't count on training them properly or having all of the needed skills to complement the entire group and ensure a successful capture (an expert marksman, Tracker, roper, and animal handler, for example). In a few cases, he knew such professionals, but in many others he could never really get to know them as professional man-hunters, nor develop them as a cohesive team. And I am convinced he would never entrust his life to a green, temporary deputy unless his back was truly against the wall. In fact, some of the most historically successful posses of the Old West were Texas Rangers and elite members of the US Marshal's Service who were well trained, well equipped, and highly sought after for the pursuit and apprehension of dangerous outlaws.

Today's successful operations are no different.

No matter which of the below mentioned units you are affiliated with, you can enhance your skill at tracking humans within the countersurveillance, counter-improvised explosive devices of all sorts, perimeter security, combat, reconnaissance and tracking patrols.

Below are units and organizations that have and will benefit from the skill of Human Tracking:

- combat engineers
- EOD personnel
- conventional infantry
- ground Special Operational Force elements within Special Operations Command
- Infantry Rangers
- law enforcement at the local, county and state levels
- military intelligence
- military police
- personnel recovery (search and rescue)
- reconnaissance and Long Range Surveilance units
- scouts and snipers
- Survival Evasion Resistance and Escape Training program
- Texas Rangers
- US Marshals
- USMC combat hunter program
- unmanned vehicle systems personnel
- weapons intelligence teams
- US Air Force Para Rescue Units

So before you saddle up your horses and ride to the rescue of a lost person or damsel in distress captured by the evil villain, know the

Figure 7.1 Tracking team. The author with Philippine Trackers.

fundamentals taught in this book and put them into action during training. If you and your tracking team want to be more than just average at this business of following a trail, you must train together (figure 7.1). By this, I don't mean that you go out in the woods a couple times a year and practice trailing a deer. I mean that every available opportunity you have, you need to spend the weekend in the mountains, in the desert, in the rain forest, trailing a volunteer "Chase" or opposing forces (OPFOR) team to hone your skills to their sharpest levels.

The US Army has a saying, "Train as you will fight." That means re-create actual battlefield conditions as closely as you possibly can. If you will be depending on your buddy in a life-and-death situation, learn to depend on him daily during less hazardous conditions. Develop a trust that cannot be broken in day-to-day activities, and it will rise to the occasion when it is really needed.

For a tracking team, the same is true. If you have the luxury of training together daily or near daily, take advantage of the situation. If you can only train once or twice a month, by all means do it. The key here is to get to know your team members. Discover each member's likes, dislikes, strengths, and weaknesses; learn one another's idiosyncrasies during times of ease as well as stress; eat together, sleep together, and train together to such a degree that you know one another's individual and collective responsibilities, probable reactions, and even thought patterns. Work on developing trust in little things and in training simulations, so that when it really counts, you can depend on your team.

For some agencies, such cohesiveness in training becomes difficult to attain because of each team member's regular job responsibilities. I of all people surely understand the challenges of these circumstances, but every effort must be taken to train in this area of your chosen profession, if you want to be successful.

Whether the organization consists of the Drug Enforcement Agency countering a narco-guerrilla ground operation in South America/Southeast Asia, the Federal Bureau of Investigation becoming involved in a massive manhunt in North Carolina, or a military unit dealing with ground operations, it is the reconnaissance, scout sniper, and tracker teams that are the tip of the spearhead for these initiatives.

TRACKER TEAM

So what does the ideal tracker team look like? What does it consist of?

The answer—and you already know what I'm going to say—depends on the mission and the purpose of the team. A hostile pursuit tracking team will look and act differently than a search and rescue team. Even though they have the same mission—finding and bringing back the Chase—their methods, equipment, and team makeup will be entirely different. A military team may want to minimize its size, in order to maintain noise discipline, camouflage, and secrecy. It will also have been trained in the various aspects of F3-EAD: *finding* (enemy combative or fugitive); *fixing* on their location; *finishing* them off (capturing or killing); *exploiting* their action; analyzing their activity; and *disseminating* the information. A search and rescue team, on the other hand, may welcome the addition of fifty volunteers, if they can be of real assistance in finding little Johnny.

For most purposes covered in this book, the ideal size of a tracking team is four, maybe five at the most, consisting of a Tracker, coverman/second Tracker, team leader/communications specialist, and rear security/medic/EMT. The fifth person may provide additional flank security or communications, while carrying some of the operational equipment to lighten the load on others. If this person does not possess competent medical skills, I would place him as rear security and place the medic near the team leader. Since each individual's responsibilities differ during a hostile pursuit from those in a nonhostile pursuit, I will cover both scenarios separately.

Duties and Responsibilities

Tracker. The primary purpose of the Tracker is, you guessed it, to look for and interpret signs left by the Chase. But the job goes well beyond this limited definition. In fact, it is closely related to that of point man in a military operation.

The experienced lead Tracker and the point man are always cognizant of the opposition by means of their own intuition and/or indicators (signs) left by the Chase. Both are aware of their surroundings. The difference between the Tracker and the point man is the path or route each walks. The path of the point man is preplanned, charted, and chosen with the belief that it is the most tactically sound passage to the advantage of the team and disadvantage of the opposing force. The path of the Tracker, on the other hand, is subject to the cunning of the Chase. Maybe the Chase selected his path with a contingency plan in the event he may be pursued. This contingency may be to deceive, harass, delay, or illuminate any Trackers in pursuit by means of booby trapping and/or ambushing the Tracker or tracking team.

I cannot stress enough that if the team is shadowing or following in hot pursuit of a hostile Chase, the primary role of Trackers is *to ensure their area of responsibility is clear of the presence of any hostile opposition before committing themselves and their teammates through the path of the chased.* Therefore, the Tracker controls the rate of movement throughout the entire chase, depending on what types of signs the Chase leaves in his wake.

As a young instructor, I was taught these lessons by a gunnery sergeant, a veteran of Vietnam, in the Northern Training Area of Okinawa as part of our counterinsurgency training. This same process was confirmed to me at a 1994 Malaysian tracking course taught by a Malaysian Tracker who pursued insurgent guerrillas. Additionally, they taught me the value of the "Don'ts" of tracking. They are:

1. Don't bluff yourself by imagining signs (be true to yourself).

2. Don't track when you are tired (unless you want to spring a booby trap or get killed in an ambush).

3. Don't make noise, and observe only the highest standards of fieldcraft.

4. Don't leave too many signs, such as breaking leaves or twigs.

5. Don't merely observe the ground immediately in front of you. Signs are everywhere. Remember, there are top, middle, and ground signs.

The Tracker normally accomplishes the job by utilizing a predetermined set of procedures known as the "Tracker Observation Procedures." The use of the Tracker Observation Procedures will enable you to follow your Chase's path with more caution as well as confidence. There are two types of Tracker Observation Procedures, one geared toward the hostile Chase, the other for a nonhostile Chase.

Hostile Chase. During a hostile pursuit, while following a hostile Chase, the Tracker Observation Procedures consists of eight phases, as follows:

Phase 1: Look for signs of the opposition. This is accomplished by identifying the farthest recognizable sign, looking around your immediate area from a stationary position out to the terrain surrounding the sign, and then carrying the search beyond the sign to detect the presence of the opposition. By probing these areas with your senses of sight, hearing, smell, touch, and intuition, you will not only be able to foil any cunning actions your opposition may employ, but you will aid yourself in expediting Phase 2.

The Tracker is the person who is out front; he is the one who can see the farthest; and he is normally the one who will identify signs of the opposition before other team members can. It's not that he is any better than the other team members, he just has a better opportunity than they do to discover opposing personnel.

All team members' eyes—figuratively speaking—are on the Tracker during this most important security scan. His signal will determine their formation, their level of relaxation or watchfulness, and their weapons readiness. Conversely, the very lives of his team members rest on the shoulders of the Tracker during this phase of the Tracker Observation Procedures, and he must never forget that.

Once he is assured that there are no hostile personnel in the immediate area, the Tracker can commence the next phase.

Phase 2: Determine all possible directions of movement your Chase may have taken (see chapter 5, under Direction of Movement). If you have been following a clear set of footprints for 100 meters, you may feel fairly comfortable with the fact that your Chase is traveling in the same direction you've been. But the key thing to remember in a hostile chase is, expect the unexpected. How sure are you that the Chase hasn't actually been walking backward to deceive you and the team? Maybe the Chase made a circular route that will actually drive the team into an ambush. At this point in the Tracker Observation Procedures, consider *all* possible directions that the Chase may have taken.

To do this, make a map reconnaissance. Ask yourself, "Where might this Chase be going?" If tactically feasible, call in for backup, placing a team either at an ambush site or on a listening/observation post. Call in for direct or indirect fire support by calling for mortar, artillery, close air support, or naval gunfire. These types of supporting fire can kill, harass, or deny the Chase's probable route or mission site. Depending on weather, terrain, adjacent friendly elements, or your own position, "walk in" these fire support missions by creeping rounds toward the Chase from the opposite direction of his movement. By your denying his direction of movement and any avenue of escape, he will be forced to return through his initial route, where your team can ambush, kill, or capture him. In the same way, law enforcement agencies can block the Chase's avenue of approach by strategically placing either helicopters or teams ahead of him.

Phase 3: Rule out possible directions of movement. During this phase, you narrow down the possibilities. If there is a sheer cliff to the immediate west with no signs of ropes, rock climbing equipment, or disturbance of nature, you can most likely rule out that area as a possible direction of travel. If the area to the east of you consists of tall, thick, overlapping blackberry bushes, which show no sign of disturbance or passage through them, you can also rule that direction out, at least for the time being. (Of course, if the trail dead-ends a few meters up the road, you may want to come back and take a much closer look at those innocent-looking blackberry bushes.)

Narrow down all the possible directions of travel to the most likely directions taken, and then make an educated determination on which one the Chase took.

Phase 4: Align yourself with the farthest sign and the path you are traveling. The line won't always be straight ahead and may even zigzag in an attempt to throw off the pursuit. The important thing here is to determine the *most likely* direction of travel, as that will serve as your starting point in locating the next sign.

Once you have aligned yourself, take a mental note of the direction of movement and, if need be, shoot an azimuth in line with the direction of travel.

Phase 5: Confirm or deny possible anti-tracking. Look closely at the signs before you. Look to your left and right to confirm or deny any assumption that the opposition may have used an anti-tracking technique or tactic to deceive you, hide from you, or delay, booby trap, or ambush you. Is the stride the same length as when you first discovered and measured it? Are the toe marks a little too pronounced? Are there pointers to your left or right? Use the techniques discussed in the previous chapters to discover whether or not your Chase has attempted to deceive you.

Phase 6: Memorize the segment of the Chase's path from your current location to the point of observation of the farthest sign. In Phase 4, you made a mental note or azimuth reading of the possible direction of travel. Now, you need to memorize it. Take notice of the terrain, vegetation, and obstacles between your current location and the farthest sign. You do not want to be looking down while you take on the responsibility of and proceed as point man. In fact, you must always be looking ahead, beyond the current sign, even while approaching it and looking to see if the sign is significant. And don't forget to take note of the second, farther landmark to allow quicker realignment to your Chase's prospective path.

Phase 7: Repeat Phase 1, looking for signs of the opposition. As the phase suggests, look once again for the bad guys. You have just been distracted for some time and are about to move out. Do you really want to take that first step without making sure something hasn't changed or without ensuring you didn't miss something the first time around?

Phase 8: Become the point man. At this point, the Tracker transitions to and takes on the responsibility of point man. In a military operation, the point man is the man out front. He will be the first to see danger; he will also be the first to experience it. It goes without saying that the point man needs to maintain the utmost vigilance throughout the move forward. Since stealth is of utmost importance, this should be the first and only time movement takes place during this Tracker Observation Procedure. Even though your team members will be providing cover during your move, they will most likely not see what you do and may not see the ambush until you are in the middle of it. Comforting thought, I know.

Nevertheless, without this phase, the pursuit grinds to a halt. Presuming all goes well during your movement forward, you then take cover and provide frontal security for the other team members moving up. Be on the alert for an unexpected offensive. With the entire team moving forward and only one person—you—providing security, this is the most vulnerable time for a tracking team, and your Chase most likely knows this. (Note: While this appears to be a long and mundane process, it actually is a flowing, smooth procedure that takes less time to do than it takes to explain.)

Everyone on the team must understand and accept the times the Tracker must move forward slowly and at times nervously, striving to maintain composure in order not to alert the opposition. Many times, the opposition is either nowhere near the Tracker's immediate area or is not aware that the Tracker is shadowing or in pursuit. Unfortunately for the Tracker, most of those heart-beating, tense, adrenaline-flowing, and sweaty moments are self-imposed.

Once your team has arrived, turn over security functions to the coverman and perform the Tracker Observation Procedures to determine the next sign.

Nonhostile Chase. The Tracker Observation Procedures for a nonhostile pursuit will be somewhat similar to that of the hostile Chase, without the life-threatening dangers and the resulting precautions. Because of the lack of precautions, not only will the Tracker Observation Procedures be shorter with regards to the number of phases, they will also be less time-consuming, allowing the team to move much faster along the trail of the Chase.

Phase 1: Look for signs of the Chase. Use whatever search methods are most appropriate for the conditions, weather, and terrain, and mark the farthest sign within your search area. Immediately probe the area with your senses as well as your intuition, looking around your proximate area and beyond the farthest sign to detect the presence of your Chase. It may be that Johnny is hiding under that little outcropping of rock to the west or has climbed a tree to get away from wolves or wild boars.

If appropriate, you may even want to call out your Chase's name in the event that he is close enough to hear it. When calling out a name, however, stop, listen, look, and smell. Stop: call out his name. Listen carefully: The Chase may be weak and his voice so faint that you are unable to hear; listen for sounds other than a human voice, such as thumping, banging, or clapping. Look: Watch for movement, such as the swaying of a tree or smoke rising. Smell: Sniff the air for smoke or anything related to the Chase (fragrance, deodorant, perspiration, for example).

Phase 2: Determine the most likely directions of travel. This is accomplished in the same manner as during the hostile chase, without ruling out any prospective direction.

Phase 3: Rule out possible directions of movement. This also is done the same way as in the hostile chase, eliminating areas covered by obstacles or features that would render travel highly unlikely.

Phase 4: Align yourself with the farthest sign and the path you are traveling. This is also accomplished the same way as in the hostile chase.

Phase 5: Confirm or deny the possibility that the Chase may have wandered off track. In a search and rescue, the Chase is most likely frightened after unexpectedly finding himself in a life-threatening situation. He may not be thinking clearly; he may have put himself into a panic; he may have become disoriented due to strange terrain, unfamiliar territory, or lack of wilderness training. He may have been overcome with fatigue or a sense of fatality, leaving the established path to find shelter, flag down an airplane, or sit down and rest for a while. It is imperative at this point that you look carefully for any signs of wandering, as a passed pathway could spell disaster for the lost person. Once you are convinced that you did not miss such a sign, move on to the next phase.

Phase 6: Move forward to the farthest sign and repeat Phase 1 actions to discover the next sign.

When reading the Tracker Observation Procedures, you may think it seems to be some mundane process that will delay you every time you go through each phase. Initially, this procedure *will* delay you. Nonetheless, it is important that you follow these procedural phases by exercising them until they become second nature, as natural as blinking your eyes. In due time, the whole process will take but a quick glance, allowing you to move at a confident, fast, yet safe pace with minimum interruption of your movement.

Track Searching Procedures

During the course of any pursuit, you will most likely come across a time when you have—Heaven forbid!—lost the path of your Chase. In this event, you will have to take steps to reestablish the direction of travel and relocate the Chase's path. There are four procedures that you can use at this point, each with its own varying degree of success. Just remember, before you start any of them during the course of a hostile pursuit, inform your coverman of your intentions so he can get himself into a high-security state of mind and prepare appropriately.

Probing Procedure: This procedure is normally the first one tried and is similar to taking a rod and prodding a haystack until it hits whatever—or whomever—is inside. Except in this case, you are the rod, and you are probing outward from your location.

This procedure is used the moment you are unable to find any sign of your Chase's path and is started by returning to the last confirmed sign. Mark it in an obvious, distinguishable manner that you can easily recognize. Probe (move) forward slowly and meticulously in the most likely area in which a sign could be placed. Subject to the vegetation and terrain, the probe should be carried out approximately three to six meters from the sign. Look closely for any new signs. If you find any that can be confirmed beyond a doubt, commence Phase 1 of the Tracker Observation Procedures.

If you do not find any new signs, return to the last confirmed sign, turn approximately 45 degrees in either direction, and probe forward again. If you do not find any new signs, return to the last confirmed sign, turn forty-five degrees in the opposite direction from the first time, and probe forward once again (see figure 7.2). If you still have not found evidence of any new signs, commence the Initial Search Procedure.

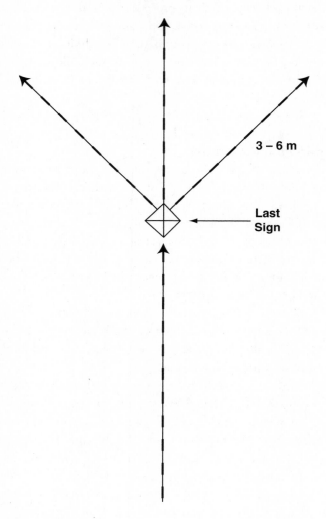

Figure 7.2 Probing procedure.

Initial Search Procedure: The purpose of this procedure is to narrow down the possible directions of movement and rule out possible deception.

The first step in this procedure is to return, you guessed it, to the last confirmed sign facing the previous direction of travel. At this point, turn around (you know, do an about-face, make a 180-degree turn). Backtrack the Chase's path; however, do not travel on the same path, but instead *parallel* the path. Go a distance of about six to twelve meters (again, depending on the terrain and vegetation) and make a wide sweeping circle around the sign in either direction, maintaining an equal distance all the way around the previous sign (see figure 7.3). If another sign is discovered, determine how this new sign lines up with the previous last confirmed sign and either conduct Phase 1 of the Tracker Observation Procedures or initiate the Probing Procedure to see whether or not the Chase has changed direction.

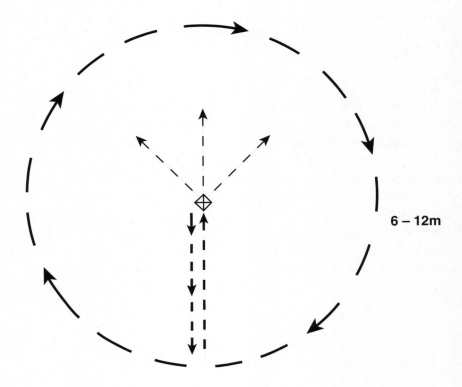

Figure 7.3 Initial search procedure.

Whether the direction of movement has changed or not, you must rule out any intention the Chase may have had. There is a possibility that the Chase may have gone to a harbor site (sleeping site). There is a possibility that the Chase may have conducted an anti-tracking tactic by splitting up, to make it more difficult to locate more than one person. Understandably, you should not take off following the first sign you discover. To rule out these possible intentions, as well as those unknown to you, finish your initial searching drill.

If unable to discover a new sign, return to the last confirmed sign and commence the Extended Search Procedure.

Extended Search Procedure: This method takes the steps from the first two procedures and broadens the geographic area further. Return back to the last confirmed sign, make a 180-degree turn, backtrack the Chase's path on a parallel path out to a distance of twelve to eighteen meters, and circle the last confirmed sign in either direction, maintaining the appropriate distance. I must emphasize here that the depth of the extended search is based on the weather, terrain, vegetation, and hostility (or lack of hostility) of your Chase.

Once a new sign is discovered, see how it lines up with the previous last confirmed sign. Conduct Phase 1 of the Tracker Observation Procedures and/or the Probing Procedure to determine whether or not the Chase has gone a different direction and to search for a new sign.

If no new sign is found, use your best deductive reasoning to determine the most likely location that a desperate person in your Chase's condition would go—then search that location or place surveillance on it.

Note: If dealing with a hostile Chase during any of the search procedures, the rest of the team should be at a 100-percent defensive alert. Before the Tracker and coverman depart, a contingency plan should be left with the team leader, in the event something threatening takes place against the team or the Tracker and coverman during the search. While in the military, I was always given a five-point contingency, consisting of the following:

1. Where is the departing element going?

2. Who is leaving?

3. How long will they be gone before linking up with the parent unit?

4. What is to happen if the departing element does not return or link up?

5. What action will the parent unit and/or departed element take in the event of enemy contact?

Although the Tracker is cognizant of the defenseless posture he places himself in during the search, he is assured that the coverman will safeguard his life. It is during these moments in the time of a tracker team, or any team in similar circumstances, that the very foundation of the word "cohesiveness" is optimized and brought to life. As my life is dependent on my team, so my team's lives are dependent on mine. There is no greater love.

Most Probable Search Area: If you are down to this last procedure, your Chase has most likely shaken you through the application of a deceptive technique, and you most likely have no idea where he or they have gone. This deceptive technique will either award the Chase time to greater distance himself from you and eventually lose you, or it could eliminate the tracker team. If the personnel is available and planned correctly, the Most Probable Search Area can be used in conjunction with the pursuit of your Chase.

The Most Probable Search Area consists simply of looking in areas the Chase would most likely go to or use. These include shelters, such as bridges, caves, probable camping sites, barns, stables, or sheds; pathways, such as roads, railroad tracks, stream banks, riverfronts, embankments, and junctions (look for prints in shallow water and rocks; search for stirred-up mud and splattered rocks); targets for sabotage or reconnoitering, such as national monuments, industrial areas, dams, bridges, or popular landmarks; or other areas, such as gradual steep slopes. Depending on the desired end result, other resources—satellite imagery, boats or watercraft, drones, or the like—can without a doubt assist in the manhunt.

With your skill, intuition, and determination, one of these methods is bound to work.

Coverman (Hostile Chase)/Second Tracker (Nonhostile Chase). The coverman or second Tracker is the second-most important member of the tracking team. In fact, the Tracker and the coverman are a team within a team, as these are the two that need to understand each other implicitly. With a relationship of unquestionable trust, they need to know when the other is stressed, fatigued, worried, or sharp.

The coverman receives information conveyed by the Tracker; the coverman forwards this information to the team leader. While the primary concern of the rest of the team is flank and rear security, this two-man tracking team provides maximum security to the front. While maintaining frontal security, they are ensuring that the team is not funneled into a booby trap lane or an ambush alley. The coverman takes the second-most stressful job.

In a hostile pursuit, the coverman does just what the name implies: He covers the Tracker throughout the Tracker Observation Procedures and/or during the Track Search Procedures (see figure 7.4). He is the one

Figure 7.4 Tracking team in action. Coverman and Tracker performing TOP.

who needs to be ever sharp and aware of their surroundings, ready to react at a moment's notice or at the first sign of danger. He is the eyes and ears of the Tracker when the Tracker is otherwise occupied and distracted.

The coverman must employ all of his senses, not to locate signs, but to discover evidence of the opposition—before *they* discover the tracking team. His focus is to the front and the sides to prevent the Tracker or the team from walking into an ambush.

Let's make one thing perfectly clear: It is extremely important that the coverman refrain from doing the Tracker's job. If he does so, he will fail at his, and such an error could cost the life of the Tracker, himself, or the entire team. There are times when the Tracker is so tense, he may overlook a deceptive ploy the Chase may have initiated. Therefore, the coverman must be relaxed, looking to his immediate frontal right and left for signs of deception. Each individual must focus on his particular job: the Tracker on finding signs and direction of movement; the coverman on discovering and preventing harm from the opposition.

Outside of his protective duties, the coverman is also the second Tracker. He must be equally or nearly as knowledgeable and experienced as the primary Tracker, since he will be the one to take over the duties when the primary Tracker needs a break. He therefore needs to be cognizant of what the Tracker is doing at all times, keeping up to date with the signs found, the direction of travel, the dangers involved, and the methods employed thus far to find the Chase.

The second Tracker must be able to recognize when the primary Tracker needs to be relieved. He needs to know the signs of fatigue or injury, even if the primary Tracker attempts to hide them; he needs to keep track of the time, ensuring that the Tracker does not spend any more than four consecutive hours on intense trailing—especially if not acclimated—before he is pulled back to assume coverman, flank, or rear security duties. Any margin of error, due to fatigue of the Tracker, can place the entire team on a booby trap lane, in an ambush alley, or on a wild goose chase. One should not track when exhausted.

Additionally, the second Tracker and/or radio operator is the recorder. He is the one who writes down the azimuths, distance traveled, obstacles encountered, and changes in direction. This responsibility can be split between two individuals: The radio operator can record route information, and the coverman can record signs or information found. Although everyone is responsible for regular navigational checks, the coverman and Tracker should discuss any changes that may develop, especially if the Chase is projecting, by means of his signs, an intention that may warrant speed or the augmentation of an additional team to cut him off or watch him. The coverman may even be the one to take photographs, shoot a video, or sketch a rough picture of the signs encountered while the Tracker is collecting and preserving them.

No matter which role he assumes at any give time, he must keep in constant contact with the Tracker, ready to take over primary tracking duties at a moment's notice.

Team Leader. The person most senior in rank, status, or experience is most often designated the team leader. This is the person who makes the decisions and maintains control at all times; this is the person who pulls the team together, trains them, and turns them into the cohesive, close-knit crew they should be. This should not be a person who is thrown into the position at the last minute just because he is senior. Experience is the number one criteria.

Before the team ever sets foot in the woods on a live mission, the team leader should be preparing his crew. He is the one who should be planning, executing, participating, and evaluating training that should be as realistically difficult as the prospective missions they may be called upon to accomplish. If the team anticipates hostile missions, for example, the team leader should be arranging for simulated opposition forces to harass, ambush, or set booby traps for the tracking team during training exercises (see Training for the Beginning Tracker, in this chapter). Standard operating procedures (SOPs) must be established.

During actual missions, the team leader assumes the overall responsibility for the success or failure of the search. He places himself centrally where he can easily maintain control, security, and command of his team. During hostile movement, he will be the one (or one of two) to provide flank security.

Throughout the conduct of the pursuit, he must keep the tracking team updated, providing status of the Chase, situational changes, and plans for the next step. He needs to ensure that each team member knows what to do from start to finish, at any given time, and during any anticipated action. He must provide them with grid coordinates, maps, and methods to find their current location, destinations, or reconnoiter areas; he must cover return methods and routes; and he must ensure they all know their PACE (Primary, Alternate, Contingency, and Emergency plans), including the courses of action for these plans.

Throughout the conduct of the operation, the team leader must maintain communication with higher headquarters or the higher command. This used to be almost exclusively by radio, but today he may communicate via cell phone, satellite phone, palm pilot, or even laptop, sending e-mails to the headquarters base camp or command post. Of course, during a military operation, the team leader must use only secure, or encrypted, methods of communication, as approved by the Department of Defense.

On a daily basis, either at the end of the day or at a predetermined time of day (presumably when the daily search has concluded, while not setting a pattern), he will submit a Situation Report, also known as a SITREP (see appendix F). On a tracking patrol when the likelihood of chance contact is probable to imminent, when immediate contact is made, a SALT Report is the first report that will be sent to higher (see appendix G). During or immediately after unforeseen yet anticipated incidences with the opposition, he will submit a hasty report, known in the Army as the SALUTE Report (which stands for Size, Activity, Location, Uniform, Time, and Equipment) (see appendix H). If in a hostile pursuit, everyone should be well-versed in a nine-line Medevac Report (see appendix I). If during a search, an improvised explosive device (IED) is found a nine-line IED Report is to be submitted (see appendix J).

And finally, at the end of the operation or during team handover, the team leader will prepare and present the formal Tracking Patrol Report. He will gather the pertinent information from the Tracker and coverman/second Tracker, which they have been gathering along the way, condense it into bite-size chunks, and present it in verbal and/or written form to the higher command or to the team taking over operations (see Tracking Patrol Report, previous chapter).

Rear Security/Designated Medic or EMT. Last but not least is the person (or persons) who makes up the rear security (in a hostile chase) or provides the medical aid. This individual is not just "following the leader." He also has very distinct and important responsibilities.

During a hostile pursuit, he is the one who ensures that no enemy or opposition comes up secretly behind the team or follows them. He not only has to keep an eye to his front, watching where the team is going, he also has to keep looking back, scanning all areas to the rear.

Besides being schooled in rear security, this individual must also be well trained in the art of anti-tracking. This is because his second responsibility is to cover the signs produced and left by his own team members. A team of four or five members is not going to trudge through the woods without notice. Even the most stealthy and highly trained teams are going to leave some kind of evidence that they passed through the area, although intense training can alleviate much of this. It is up to the last individual to cover up these marks, replace displaced foliage, and obscure prints left by many soles, so that a Chase circling around behind will not have a path the size of the Oregon Trail to follow.

In a nonhostile chase, this last individual will most likely be the designated medic, EMT, or first-aid person. He or she should be a trained EMT, or at least schooled or certified in advanced first aid and CPR. This person will carry all first-response first-aid supplies, which should handle bites or injuries most likely to be encountered in that geographic area, with its unique foliage, insects, animal population, and terrain. The designated medic should also prepare a small first-aid kit for each team member.

He will also need to be prepared to treat the Chase when he is found. A hostile Chase may have bullet wounds, knife cuts, or myriad other conditions or injuries. A search and rescue victim may additionally have broken bones, but he may also have received insect stings, animal bites, or rashes/welts from poisonous plants; he may be suffering from exposure, frostbite, serious sunburn, or dehydration; he may need prescription medication (which can be provided by family members) to counter the effects of diabetes, mental illness, AIDS, or other potentially life-threatening conditions. And the medic should always be prepared to deal with a heart condition and/or shock. It is up to the team medic to research the Chase's needs and obtain the necessary items. Overall, his purpose is to sustain life until the patient is handed over to a physician.

Depending on the amount of weight he is already carrying, he may also want to include a few comfort items for the Chase, especially in the case of a lost child. Maybe little Johnny has a favorite teddy bear, brand of candy, security blanket, religious article, or another memento that will give him immediate consolation when he is found.

Others. If other people are included on the team, there are roles that they can fill. On a five-person team, the fifth person can be the radio operator, communications specialist, or route recorder, helping the team leader maintain contact with higher headquarters or base camp. The team leader may feel the need for an additional medic or for a member who can provide supplementary security on the flanks or in the rear. However many people make up the team, they can all share part of the load, transporting items that help the designated team members carry out their regular duties more easily.

As I said in the first part of this chapter, the optimum size of a tracking team is four or five. Any more than that, and the team runs the risk of either exposing itself to a hostile Chase or inadvertently destroying valuable signs that could direct it to the lost person it is desperately trying to find before nightfall.

Formations

So now that we know the makeup of the optimum team, what type of formations should they be in to effectively pursue a Chase while the team leader ensures the security, stealth, control, flexibility, and accountability of the tracking team? Obviously, for a nonhostile Chase, no real formation is necessary, other than getting in line shoulder to shoulder, the distance between team members dependent upon terrain, weather, vegetation, and time. This is perfectly acceptable as long as the team leader can effectively control the team, and as long as team members perform their responsibilities without interfering with the primary Tracker and second Tracker. Area searches can also be conducted under nonhostile conditions with the aid of helicopters and boats searching the contour of the earth at low levels. Tracker Observation Procedures and Tracker Search Procedures may remain the same.

There are three main formations my team and I have used over the years, which are of great value for the quick reaction of a small fire and maneuver element: the File, the V, and the Wedge. The type of formation used and the distance between team members will be based on the exact mission, the terrain, vegetation, weather, the Chase, team member strengths and weaknesses, and time available to complete the operation. The distance is also dependent upon how the team leader can best control and direct his team while maintaining security, the effectiveness of the pursuit, and the formation with no break in contact between team members for accountability purposes.

File. This movement is normally used in limited-visibility weather; heavy, dense vegetation; and/or steep terrain that allows little room for maneuvering to either side of the main trail. This formation is just what it indicates. It is a single-file formation, led off by the Tracker, then the coverman, team leader, communication specialist, and the first-aid medic/rear security (see figure 7.5). Each person has a responsibility for covering some portion of the perimeter, as discussed earlier in this chapter. In this formation, the Tracker will cover the area to his immediate front; the coverman will cover the area to his front and on either side of the Tracker, the team leader to one flank (or both flanks in a four-person team), the communications specialist the other flank, and the rear security the area to the rear of the formation. While not the most secure formation, it is the most feasible and allows for maximum speed in tight areas. Collectively, 360-degree security is maintained. Individually, the Tracker and rear security each have an approximate 230-degree field of fire; all other team members have 160 degrees of interlocking fire to their flanks. This type of formation is easy to control.

Vee or V. This type of formation, which actually looks more like a Y than a V, allows for maximum security while on the move and is used in moderate vegetation with flat to rolling terrain when contact is imminent. In this instance, the Tracker takes a secondary role, giving way to not one, but two covermen who provide security to the front and on either side,

Figure 7.5 File formation.

making the top ends of the V. The Tracker completes the bottom of the V formation, followed by the team leader and rear security in a line directly behind. The team leader now must provide flank security on both sides of the team, while the rear security protects the area in back of the team (see figure 7.6). This formation is slower and slightly more difficult to control,

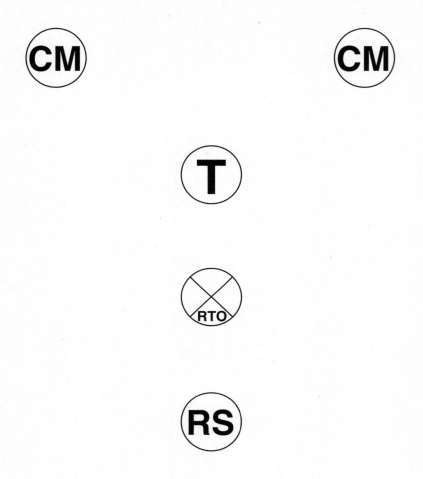

Figure 7.6 Vee or V formation.

but if well rehearsed and included as part of the SOP, control will be no problem.

In the V formation, the collective 360-degree security is not compromised. The left coverman (assuming a northward direction of travel) has a field of fire that starts at 80 degrees and shifts north, west, south, and a little toward the east to 175 degrees; his total field of fire is approximately 265 degrees. The right coverman does the same on the right side of the formation and has approximately the same 265-degree field of fire on the opposite side. The covermen can have fields of fire ranging from the front of the opposing coverman to the right or left flank of the rear security. The Tracker, on the other hand, has a field of fire ranging from the right shoulder of the left coverman to the left shoulder of the right coverman, a distance of about 90 degrees. From the rear of the covermen, the Tracker has a field of fire of approximately 110 degrees on both flanks. All other team members in front of the rear security have fields of fire of about 160 degrees to either flank. The rear security has an arc from the right shoulder of the right coverman to the left shoulder of the left coverman around the rear of the formation, representing an approximately 270-degree field of fire. Through this formation and the interlocking fields of fire, the Chase's hasty ambushes can be foiled, and sometimes deceptive counter-tracking techniques or tactics can be sighted preemptively.

Wedge. The Wedge is an inverted or upside down V, used when the team is in a sparse to open danger area, unprotected by vegetation or terrain. While still led by the Tracker, the remainder of the team is staggered down the right and left legs of the formation. The purpose of this is to provide effective protection (known as fields of fire in the military) that crisscrosses with minimal blockage of one team member's view over another's (see figure 7.7). In this formation, 360-degree security, both collectively and individually, is maximized, reducing the chance of friendly fire. This formation allows for speed and is easy to control.

Bounding Overwatch. While not a formation, this is a movement technique usually used in conjunction with the File or Wedge formations, in rolling hills and among numerous obstacles when the team is blatantly exposed and contact is imminent.

The team is divided into an A Team and a B Team, with the Tracker moving forward with whichever team is moving to the front. If this is not feasible, the team leader will designate two Trackers and perform the Bounding Overwatch in a split-team fashion. There will also be times when team members may have to move singly due to the lack of cover and concealment.

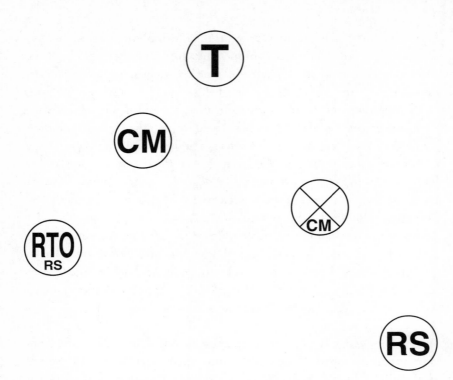

Figure 7.7 Wedge formation.

The Bounding Overwatch movement technique can be conducted successively or in an alternating fashion.

Alternating Bounds. One team (A Team) provides an overwatch position, which is a covered position that provides suppressive fire toward the opposition in the event the moving element is under fire. The other team (B Team) and the Tracker move forward to assume an overwatch position in front of the A Team. Once the B Team is in position, the A Team then moves forward to the front of the B Team, picking up the Tracker as they pass by. In this instance, only one team is moving at a time while the other is providing the maximum security possible for the other team and the Tracker (see figure 7.8). The alternating bounds are faster than successive

**Alternating
Bounds**

**Successive
Bounds**

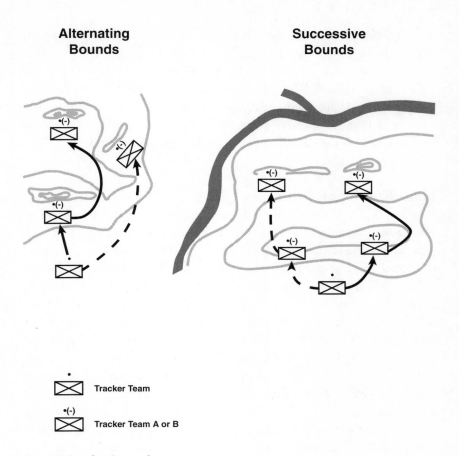

Tracker Team

Tracker Team A or B

Figure 7.8 Bounding Overwatch.

bounds. Use the alternating method only if and when the stationary over-watch team can observe the bounding team pass by and assume the over-watch position. This method will be continually used until determined unnecessary.

Successive Bounds. The A Team, with the Tracker, will move to an overwatch position. Once the overwatch position is secured, the B Team either moves to the right or left on line. Then the A Team and the Tracker move ahead to another overwatch position. This method of bounding will continue until determined unnecessary. Successive bounds are simpler to control.

Other formations may provide the same kind of security while allowing the Tracker to continue doing his job, but these are the ones I have found to be the most effective in a potentially hostile situation. Unless the Chase you are following has demonstrated the potential to harm innocent bystanders, noncombatants, or civilians, your main purpose is to provide security and safety for the tracking team while moving as quickly as possible to intercept the Chase, in order to safeguard any victims.

Immediate Action Drills

It is important to briefly discuss what is known in the US Army as "Immediate Action Drills." Due to the inherent hazards of the Trackers' profession, especially in a hostile environment, the tracker team must have the upper hand on the opposition. With minimum commands and signals, rapid action must be taken, and this is usually done by means of Immediate Action Drills, one of the first things taught to me in basic infantry training. By my gunnery sergeant's definition, which did not mince words, Immediate Action Drills "will save your a— because they provide swift and *incontestable* reaction to the enemy's physical or visual contact." They are designed to provide a quick, automatic response to predetermined situations that could otherwise prove fatal for you or the entire team.

These drills are very familiar and widely used throughout the military and a number of law enforcement agencies. Among the most common are the following:

1. Evade contact

2. Attack

3. React to contact

4. React to near and far ambushes

5. React to indirect fire

6. Air defense

The success of any mission throughout history has depended on how well the participants have rehearsed for that mission; the same can be said today and well into the future. Coming home alive from that mission, however, may well depend upon how well you have rehearsed your Immediate Action Drills.

Because the tracker team must collectively outperform the opposition deceptively, defensively, evasively, and offensively, these drills will be, without a doubt, instrumental in achieving this upper hand and saving lives. Just as your formations, movement techniques, search drills, observation procedures, and tracking reports must be part of your SOPs, you must also add Immediate Action Drills. They *must* be included in team SOPs, regularly rehearsed, *and rehearsed intensely* to the point that they become second nature. Once out in the field in the heat of battle, there is no time to stop and think about what to do under certain conditions; you need to be ready to execute at a moment's notice.

Booby Traps

Keep in mind, however, that the Chase is not likely to lie down and let you overtake him, especially if he is a dangerous fugitive, infiltrator, terrorist, guerrilla, or regular enemy soldier. In fact, he may be well-versed in laying booby traps to welcome you and your team. Terrorists and guerrilla fighters throughout history and up to the present time have been very effective in this method of warfare, and it is imperative that you be able to recognize the types of booby traps and their indicators. Remember, you are walking in the Chase's path, and you must be mentally one step ahead of him, his cunning, and his ability to deceive, delay, demoralize, or kill you.

It is important that you have a basic understanding and a high level of respect for these devices in order to avoid becoming a casualty of them.

The first thing to understand about booby traps is the reason they are effective. They are not necessarily intended to kill their victims; rather, their intention is to instill fear, suspicion, and uncertainty in the minds of those potentially vulnerable to them. It is psychological warfare that then becomes a combat multiplier, which is a great ally to physical warfare.

Booby traps are used in all three warfare operations, including defensive, offensive, and withdrawal operations. These can be conventional military devices with infrared-sensitive, high-tech microchips and remote-command detonations; or they can be unconventional, rough, improvised devices made with mostly natural vegetation and materials on hand. In either event, 99 percent of all booby traps operate by one of the following methods.

Delay: These devices have fuses that have some kind of automatic delay feature. This delay could be a stopwatch-style counter, digital countdown clock, alarm clock, or other mechanical delay, similar to a wind-up clock.

Pressure: This type of booby trap is detonated by direct pressure or by the distribution of weighted pressure on the fuse or device itself.

Pull: This is activated by pulling a trip wire away from the device.

Release: Once the weight of an individual or vehicle is distributed onto the device, it clicks the fuse or circuit partially into place. When the pressure on the device is released, the circuit is complete, and the device explodes. This was one of the favorite detonation methods in Vietnam (and is still a favorite in guerrilla warfare), combining both physical and psychological warfare most effectively. Ground troops on patrol could often hear the click of the partial detonation, realizing their doom with little or no recourse to prevent the fatal outcome.

All of these types of devices have indicators that at least partially identify them and allow the tracking team to take defensive measures against them. Watch carefully for these indicators and warnings:

1. Damaged, disturbed, or transferred vegetation (foreign to the area)

2. Electronic wire

3. Loose dirt, rope, string, vines, or other kinds of wire

4. Newly filled areas of dirt
   a. Patches of clump dirt
   b. Patches of concave dirt, particularly noted after rainfall
   c. Patches of discolored dirt or vegetation

5. Plastic or cardboard materials protruding from the ground

6. The smell of explosive materials, such as sulfur, gunpowder, or fireworks

Ask locals or your counterparts about how the opposition marks their booby traps. In Asia and Central America, locals mark their booby traps with materials indigenous to that particular area in some sort of predetermined pattern. Your constant suspicion of the unusual, inquisitive learning, and experience with previously discovered markings will result in minimal casualties.

TRAINING FOR THE BEGINNING TRACKER

In order to have an effective "posse," new members must be continually brought in and trained in the techniques taught in this book. In spite of our best efforts, veteran Trackers will move on, transfer, get promoted, suffer serious injury, or retire from these types of operations. Just like in a major league sports team, "rookies" who have shown great potential must be brought into spring training and schooled in the methods employed

Figure 7.9 Tracking class.

by professionals in the field. And just as rookies do not become veterans after one year in professional-level "trenches," neither do novice Trackers become experts after one season of even the most intensive training efforts.

Nevertheless, even the most skillful Tracker has had to start somewhere (see figure 7.9).

What follows is a series of exercises designed to develop the novice Tracker's senses, sign recognition, and awareness one step at a time, each successive exercise building upon the previous ones. At the completion of these exercises, the novice Tracker should be well grounded in tracking skills and well on the way to becoming a professional in this field.

Static and Movement Observation Drills

Before I ever start teaching a student the art of tracking, I teach the art of observation, by putting Tracker Observation Procedures into practice and exercising scanning and searching methods. I do this through both static and non-static drills.

Static Display. In this drill, the trainer hides various items within a wooded area, from one foot to five meters in front of the trainee. The articles are placed at ground-, middle-, and top-sign levels in both obvious and semi-obvious locations.

The trainee is given ten minutes to eyeball the area, and then has five minutes to turn around and record what was observed and where. Initially, the trainer may want to place the items within obvious view, gradually increasing the obscurity as the trainee improves in skill.

Moving Observation Drill. In a twenty-five-meter corridor, spread various items above eye level, in the middle, and throughout the ground of the lane. Have the trainee walk at a slow patrol pace, two minutes in an open area and seven minutes in a more forested area. At no time may the trainee touch or walk toward the items. Once at the end of the corridor, allow five minutes to write down what was seen.

To maintain the integrity of these observation drills, isolate each trainee, and allow only one observer at a time within the static display area or movement observation corridor.

Once the trainee has demonstrated the capacity to be observant, it is time to move on to the tracking exercises.

Initial Exercise

The initial exercise should take place in an open dirt lot that is at least one hundred meters in length and exposed to full morning and evening sunlight, which cast long and distinct shadows.

Step 1: Traveling east to west (or west to east), one individual deliberately lays clear-cut shoe prints, preferably with waffle-type tennis shoe soles or combat boots with distinctive markings. There is no need at this time to vary the pace, add weight, or otherwise add variety to the prints. The point here is to make the prints as recognizable and distinctive as possible as a result of shadow casting from east to west or vice versa.

Once the prints are laid, have the student trail the markings, measuring both the stride and shoe print. Have the student draw a picture of the print in detail, take a picture, and/or write a description of what is observed. Then rake or sweep the lot, and repeat the exercise until the apprentice is comfortable tracking and recognizing the prints and the effects of shadow casting on the prints.

Step 2: Repeat all facets of Step 1, laying the prints north to south or south to north. This allows for a different perspective of shadow casting.

Step 3: Repeat Steps 1 and 2 with varying speeds and postures, to include running, walking backward, carrying a heavy weight, walking with a cane, and walking with a limp (see figures 7.10A and B).

Step 4: Repeat the first three steps in other terrain and times of day. Repeat them in an open sand lot, an open grass field with dew, dry and green lawns, short to long grass, wet muddy lots, and snowed-in tracts (see figures 7.11A through D). Repeat them at night, when the ambient light of the full moon casts shadows over the prints, and do so with and without binoculars and/or night vision goggles.

Step 5: Finally, repeat the entire exercise while making two sets of prints: one deliberate and obvious, and the other parallel, in the same stride, but more natural.

Figure 7.10A Various prints. Left to right: backward, normal, running, heavy load.

Figure 7.10B Various prints. Bottom to top: backward, normal, running, heavy load.

Figure 7.11A Snow—walking normally.

Figure 7.11B Snow. Left to right: walking normally, running.

Figure 7.11C Various prints in snow. Left to right: walking, running, heavy load.

Figure 7.11D Various prints in snow (different perspective). Top to bottom: walking, running, heavy load.

Forested Area Exercise

In this exercise, find a forested area with moderate vegetation that is at least 400 to 600 meters in length. If you have a class of novice or apprentice Trackers, buddy them up in two teams of two Trackers each. This exercise will teach them the different roles they may be expected to fulfill on a live mission.

From a designated starting point forward of the "tracking team," have two "Chase" team members go forward on a given azimuth for a distance of one hundred meters, leaving a trail of visible top, middle, and ground signs in every conceivable location.[28] Once the two Chases have completed the one-hundred-meter distance, have them sound off, make noise, or call on the radio to indicate that the trail has been laid. Then have the two "Trackers" commence tracking, one taking on the role of primary Tracker and the other taking on the role of the coverman or second Tracker.

Once the two teams have met up, discuss the learning points of the exercises, then have the two teams reverse roles, the Chases becoming the Trackers, and the Trackers taking on the role of the Chase, laying the trail for the next hundred meters.

It is important for the acting Chases, when laying a trail, to incorporate as many different terrain features as possible. Have them make a stream crossing, travel through deep muddy or sandy patches, climb steep hills, or work their way through thick undergrowth (even to the point of crawling or dragging themselves through). Make sure they make the exercise as realistic as possible while providing plenty of learning opportunities. As the apprentices progress, have the Chases leave increasingly obscure signs to sharpen the novice Trackers' skills.

If training only one apprentice at a time, have instructors or assistants lay the trails while the apprentice tracks alongside a seasoned Tracker, switching roles every one hundred meters. The seasoned Tracker can point out the signs along the way when in the role of primary Tracker.

Be sure to incorporate more than just visual signs into the exercise. Re-create audible and mechanical sounds during both day and night hours. Replicate authentic overnight camping sites, leaving the sites trashed with many signs and smells. Gradually, leave more obscured signs, sounds, and

---

28 Always work in a two-person buddy team. This will help in maintaining an azimuth and checking each other's re-creation of a sign. Most of all, the two-person rule ensures the safety of both team members in the event of a training accident.

smells as the student progresses from the ranks of novice ever closer to the journeyman level of experience.

The static and movement observation drills along with the actual training field exercise should be composed of objects and replicated activities that insurgents, guerrillas, and fugitives or missing persons may possess or engage in. The objects and replicated signs, tracks, and incident sites are deliberately fed to the student in their purest form, then gradually obscured and hidden from the student's senses each day. This teaching method allows the student to eventually learn to recognize objects (targets) and interpret actionable activities (intelligence) in their least ideal forms. That recognition allows the student to develop a situational awareness accentuating that all Trackers are human sensors. Being situationally aware may save the Tracker's life or the lives of others. This type of training accompanied with the laboratory site with its compartmentalized aging observations will develop the student's real-world ability to read, deduce from, and interpret what is being sensed. By being able to read, deduce from, and interpret signs, human tracks, tire tracks, and, if pack or mounted animals are involved, spoor, the student will enhance the ability to answer what are referred to in the military as a commander's critical intelligence requirements (CCIR), which will allow the student to confirm, deny, or gather intelligence in any given area of interest or law enforcement jurisdiction.

CCIR: Commander's Critical Information Requirements. These are the critical questions that a military commander needs answers to in an area of interest which drive planning of any intelligent surveillance reconnaissance. ISRs are the assets (infantry, rangers, marine force reconnaissance, scouts, snipers, all SOF) that are capable of answering the CCIR. The operations officer coordinates with the intelligence officer that tasks the ISR assets. Individuals that are part of the assets and are skilled in human tracking are best equipped to expeditiously, and more accurately answer the intelligence officer tasked to answer the CCIR.

CCIR examples can be:

1. Where are the smuggler's infiltration and exfiltration routes?

2. What type of tactics are the armed escorts and spotters for the smugglers using?

3.   Where are these smuggling teams receiving their support?

4.   Where are the smuggler's base and safe houses?

By means of some type of Tracking Patrol Report format a given organization utilizes, this information can be immediately disseminated through an accessible network like Palantir, Query Tree, or Analyst Notebook so that the data can be Exploited, Analyzed, and Disseminated (as in the last three steps of F3-EAD).

Other Skills

Because this is an instruction manual focused on the art of tracking, many other essential skills are not covered in this book. For these other skills—including land navigation, advanced first aid, and, for the hostile Chase, advanced shooting skills, hand-to-hand combat, and camouflage—I refer you to the recommended reading list at the back of this book. For the practical application of self-defense techniques, I encourage you to explore books on Brazilian jiu jitsu, Krav Maga, an Israeli martial art, and stick and knife fighting.

Remember: This book shows a fundamental method in achieving the human tracking skill. It is up to the practitioner to train, train, and train some more.

EPILOGUE

It has been a long, arduous, and, I hope, rewarding journey through the course of this book. You now have the tools to make that all-important first step toward becoming a qualified Tracker. Eventually, with dedication and time, you *will* gain experience to the point that you will be able to track a person through a wide variety of territories and conditions. I wish you the best of luck in your tracking endeavors and all the rewards that go along with the practice and the title of Tracker.

Remember to be true to yourself, and the rest will follow. May *Tracking Humans* give you the confidence you desire to effectively capture a fugitive/criminal Chase or find a lost loved one.

Happy hunting, and thank you for giving me the privilege of sharing some of my knowledge with you!

TRACKER'S CREED

I as a Tracker understand that my success depends on my *territorial* training. Under adverse weather conditions, through urban, suburban, desert, mountain, forested, jungle, and arctic climates, I as a Tracker must be *resourceful.* I as a Tracker understand that any change in a track or sign left may be a matter of life or death. With this in mind, I as a Tracker must allow my senses to *aggressively* search for those I pursue or who pursue me. I as a Tracker must be fully *conscious* of my surroundings, never overlooking any detail or taking any human indicator for granted. I as a Tracker must pursue and elude humans with *keen* insight. I as a Tracker with my *experience* and *resilient* determination will consequently *find, fix, finish, exploit, analyze,* and *disseminate* human intelligence or elude and, if need be, eliminate the Trackers that dare to pursue me.

APPENDIX A
HUMAN PROFILE CARD

1. Date and Time: _____

2. Age: _____

3. Build: _____

4. Sex: _____

5. Height: _____

6. Weight: _____

7. Ethnicity/Race: _____

8. Approximate Age of Footprint: _____

9. Location: _____

10. Direction of Movement: _____

11. Number of People: _____

12. Type of Footwear: _____

13. Given Alias to Footprint: _____

Additional Info: _____

_____

_____

_____

_____

_____

Inscribe or sketch the color of the clothing, and whatever apparel seen on person (hat, gloves, footwear, etc. . . .).

Human Print Measurement

A_____

Length of total print pattern

B_____

Width of ball pattern

C_____

Length of heel pattern

D_____

Width of heel pattern

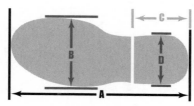

i. _____

Pitch Angles of Footprints

ii. _____

The Length of Stride

iii. _____

Width of Saddle

VEHICLE PROFILE CARD

Inscribe or sketch the color, write down the make, type of vehicle and condition, license plate number, and whatever apparel was seen on persons in the vehicle (hat, gloves, footwear, etc. . . .).

Wheel base

Year:_____ Make:_____ Type:_____

Width of Print Make:_____ Type:_____

Driver   Passenger(s)

   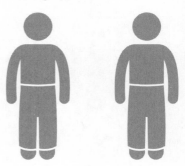

Outside-to-Outside (minus tread width)

Inside-to-Inside (minus tread width)

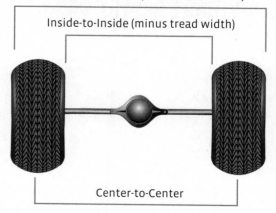

Center-to-Center

APPENDIX C
INCIDENT REPORT

INCIDENT ONE, DAY TWO   **APRIL 21, 2013**   09:30

FACTS:

AT GRID 12BDS9077580787 AN EMPTY CONTAINER WAS FOUND BY SOME
UNRECOGNIZABLE FOOTWEAR. SEE EXHIBIT ONE (a) and (b). SEVERAL PARTIAL
UNRECOGNIZABLE PRINTS WERE NOTED BUT ONE STOOD OUT THE MOST. SEE
EXHIBIT TWO (a), (b) and (C). SEE EXHIBIT THREE.

INTERPRETATION AND DEDUCTION:

THE LACK OF WEATHERING ON THE SURFACE OF THE WINTERGREEN
CONTAINER INDICATES THAT IT WAS RECENTLY EITHER INADVERTENTLY
DROPPED OR THROWN AWAY. THIS ALSO INDICATES THAT THIS PERSON MAY
HAVE A DIPPING HABIT. THIS TOBACCO CAN ONLY BE PURCHASED IN THE
UNITED STATES WHICH INDICATES THAT THE USER WAS AN AMERICAN, TOURIST,
OR A PERSON ASSOCIATED WITH THE AMERICANS. THE LABEL CLEARLY STATES
THAT THE SALE OF THIS PRODUCT CAN ONLY BE ADMINISTERED IN THE UNITED
STATES. DUE TO THE NOTABLE PRESSURE, PLACED IN THE SOIL, THE SMALL
BOOT PRINT APPEARED TO BE OF A FOREIGN MILITARY LUG/VIBRANT PATTERN.
WITH THE FOOTWEAR PATTERN BEING ELEVEN INCHES LONG, AND SHORT
STRIDE OF TWENTY-SIX INCHES WITH A NEUTRAL PITCH ANGLE INDICATED THAT
THIS WAS A SMALL PESON CARRYING HEAVY WEIGHT. THE ACTUAL PRINT WAS
A BIT WAHSED OUT DUE TO SOME RAINFALL DURING THE EARLY MORNING.
THE VEGETATION THAT POINTED IN THIS GROUP'S WESTWARD DIRECTION OF
MOVEMENT INDICATED THAT THERE WERE APPROXIMATELY TEN TO TWELVE
PERSONNEL. DUE TO A CAMERA MALFUNCTION, A PHOTO WAS NOT TAKEN.

INCIDENT REPORT

SEE EXHIBITS:

Exhibit One (a) and (b) at 12BDS9077580787

Exhibit One (a)   Exhibit One (b)

Exhibit Two (a), (b), and (c) at 12BDS9077580787
Exhibit (a)
Taken North to South from the T-intersection of the D-line toward the E-line.

INCIDENT REPORT

Exhibit Two (b)

Taken North from the E-line toward the T-intersection of the D-line.
It appears as if the boot has transferred dirt from a different location.

Exhibit Two (c)

Taken at a top view but, too overcast at the given moment and flash started malfunctioning. An artificial light could have been used to bring out the pattern when taking the photo of this exhibit, but the flashlight was in need of batteries so a sketch was drawn.

INCIDENT REPORT

Exhibit Three

Description:

The composition of the soil and low contrasting light (due to overcast conditions) exposed a distinct, lub/vibrant, footwear pattern. The pattern was a quarter of an inch deep.

      A. The pattern was eleven inches long.

      B. The ball of the footwear pattern was five inches wide.

      C. The width of the heel was three inches.

      D. The length of the heel was three inches.

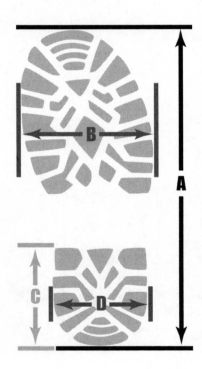

INCIDENT REPORT

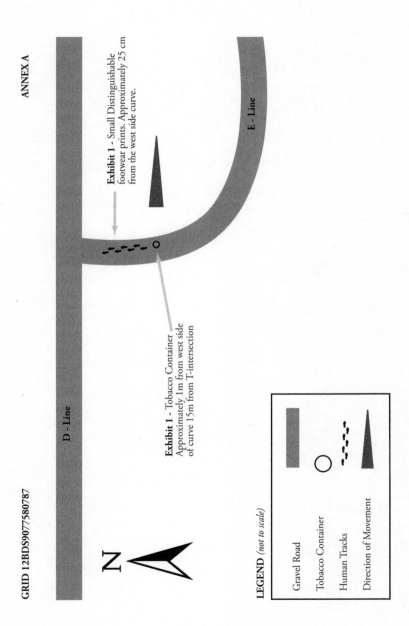

ANNEX A

GRID 12BDS9077580787

D - Line

E - Line

Exhibit 1 - Small Distinguishable footwear prints. Approximately 25 cm from the west side curve.

Exhibit 1 - Tobacco Container Approximately 1m from west side of curve 15m from T-intersection

N

LEGEND (*not to scale*)

Gravel Road

Tobacco Container

Human Tracks

Direction of Movement

INCIDENT REPORT

INCIDENT:_____   DAY:_____   DATE:_____   TIME:_____

FACTS: _____

_____

_____

_____

_____

_____

_____

_____

_____

INTERPRETATION AND DEDUCTION: _____

_____

_____

_____

_____

_____

_____

_____

SEE EXHIBIT AND ANNEX:

TRACKING PATROL REPORT

OPERATION: _____

PATROL DESIGNATION: _____

AREA OF OPERATION: _____

MAP REFERENCES: _____

PATROL COMPOSITION: _____

1. MISSION: _____

2. TIMINGS: a. Infil: _____

                      b. Exfil: _____

3. INFIL POINT: _____ METHOD: _____

4. EXFIL POINT: _____ METHOD: _____

5. GROUND:

_____
_____
_____
_____
_____
_____
_____
_____
_____
_____
_____
_____
_____
_____
_____
_____
_____
_____

DAY ONE

_____
_____
_____
_____
_____
_____
_____
_____
_____
_____
_____
_____
_____
_____
_____

DAY TWO

_____
_____
_____
_____
_____
_____
_____
_____
_____
_____
_____
_____
_____
_____
_____
_____
_____

DAY THREE

_____
_____
_____
_____
_____
_____
_____
_____
_____
_____
_____
_____
_____
_____
_____

DAY FOUR

_____
_____
_____
_____
_____
_____
_____
_____
_____
_____
_____
_____
_____
_____
_____

DAY _____

_____

_____

_____

_____

_____

_____

_____

_____

_____

_____

_____

_____

_____

_____

_____

_____

_____

DAY _____

_____

_____

_____

_____

_____

_____

_____

_____

_____

_____

_____

_____

_____

_____

_____

_____

_____

6. INTERPRETATION AND DEDUCTION:

(INTER-DEDUCTION)

INCIDENT	DAY	FACTS	INTER-DEDUCTION
_____	_____	_____	_____
		_____	_____
		_____	_____
		_____	_____
		_____	_____
		_____	_____
		_____	_____
		_____	_____
		_____	_____
		_____	_____
		_____	_____
		_____	_____
		_____	_____
		_____	_____

INCIDENT	DAY	FACTS	INTER-DEDUCTION
_____	_____	_____	_____
		_____	_____
		_____	_____
		_____	_____
		_____	_____
		_____	_____
		_____	_____
		_____	_____
		_____	_____
		_____	_____
		_____	_____
		_____	_____
		_____	_____
		_____	_____

INCIDENT	DAY	FACTS	INTER-DEDUCTION
_____	_____	_____	_____
		_____	_____
		_____	_____
		_____	_____
		_____	_____
		_____	_____
		_____	_____
		_____	_____
		_____	_____
		_____	_____
		_____	_____
		_____	_____
		_____	_____
		_____	_____
		_____	_____
		_____	_____

INCIDENT	DAY	FACTS	INTER-DEDUCTION
_____	_____	_____	_____
		_____	_____
		_____	_____
		_____	_____
		_____	_____
		_____	_____
		_____	_____
		_____	_____
		_____	_____
		_____	_____
		_____	_____
		_____	_____
		_____	_____
		_____	_____
		_____	_____
		_____	_____

INCIDENT	DAY	FACTS	INTER-DEDUCTION
_____	_____	_____	_____
		_____	_____
		_____	_____
		_____	_____
		_____	_____
		_____	_____
		_____	_____
		_____	_____
		_____	_____
		_____	_____
		_____	_____
		_____	_____
		_____	_____
		_____	_____
		_____	_____

INCIDENT	DAY	FACTS	INTER-DEDUCTION
_____	_____	_____	_____
		_____	_____
		_____	_____
		_____	_____
		_____	_____
		_____	_____
		_____	_____
		_____	_____
		_____	_____
		_____	_____
		_____	_____
		_____	_____
		_____	_____
		_____	_____
		_____	_____

7. ASSUMPTIONS:

_____
_____
_____
_____
_____
_____
_____
_____
_____
_____
_____
_____
_____
_____

8. INFORMATION GAINED:
a. Strength: _____
b. Weapons: _____
_____
_____
c. Ammunition/Demo: _____
_____
_____
d.Load/Equipment:_____
_____
_____
e. Age: Start:_____
            Finish:_____
f. Morale: _____

9. CONFIRMATION:

I-CAPTURED:_____

II-K.I.A.: _____

III-RESCUED:_____

IV-SEIZED WAS: _____

_____

a. _____

_____

b. _____

_____

c. _____

_____

d. _____

_____

e. _____

_____

f. _____

_____

g. _____

10. RECOMMENDATIONS:

a. _____

_____

b. _____

_____

c. _____

_____

d. _____

_____

LABORATORY OBSERVATION REPORT

WEATHER DATA FOR HUMAN TRACKING: **SKETCH:**

DAY:	DATE:
Location:	
Type of Aging Stand: Shelter/Unsheltered	
Speed and Direction of Wind:	
Temperature:	
Precipitation:	
Humidity:	
Cloud Coverage:	
Altitude:	
Sunrise: Sunset:	
Moonrise: Moonset:	
Moon Phase:	

DESCRIPTION:

_____
_____
_____
_____
_____
_____
_____
_____
_____
_____
_____
_____
_____
_____
_____
_____
_____
_____
_____
_____
_____
_____
_____
_____
_____
_____
_____
_____
_____
_____
_____
_____
_____
_____
_____
_____

APPENDIX F
SITUATION REPORT (SITREP)

Sent out every 24 hours as a routine report.

Line One: Location _____
_____
_____

Line Two: Strength _____
_____

Line Three: Condition (of the team)—Excellent, Good, Fair, Poor _____
_____
_____

Line Four: Oppositional Contact _____
_____

Line Five: Significant Activities _____
_____

Line Six: Projected Significant Activities _____
_____

SALT REPORT

Size: _____

_____

Activity: _____

_____

_____

Location: _____

_____

Time: _____

SALUTE REPORT

Sent out immediately after a significant incident, such as contact with opposition forces or individuals.

Size/Strength: _____

_____

Activity: _____

_____

_____

Location: _____

_____

Uniform(s): _____

_____

Time: _____

Equipment: _____

_____

_____

_____

9-LINE MEDEVAC REPORT

Line 1: Six-digit UTM grid location of pick-up site. _____

Line 2: Radio frequency, call sign and suffix of requesting personnel; encryption frequency. _____
_____
_____

Line 3: Number of patients by precedence (Urgent = loss of life or limb within two hours. Priority = loss of life or limb within four hours. Routine = evacuate within twenty-four hours.) _____
_____
_____
_____

Line 4: Special equipment required, as applicable (none, hoist, Stokes litter, or jungle penetrator). _____
_____
_____
_____

Line 5: Number of patients by type (litter, ambulatory). _____
_____
_____
_____

Line 6: Security of pick-up site (no enemy or artillery in the area; possibly enemy troops or artillery in the area [approach with caution]). _____
_____
_____
_____

Line 7: Method of marking pick-up site (branches, stones, panels, signal lamp, flashlight, smoke or pyrotechnics). _____

_____

_____

_____

Line 8: Patient nationality and status (US military, US civilian, non-US personnel or POW). _____

_____

_____

_____

Line 9: Chemical, biological, radiological, and nuclear status (CBRN contamination). _____

_____

_____

_____

APPENDIX J
9-LINE IED REPORT

Line 1: Date time group (DTG) item was discovered. _____

Line 2: Reporting activity: unit ID and location. _____
_____
_____
_____

Line 3: Contact method (radio frequency, call sign, point of contact, and telephone number)._____
_____
_____
_____

Line 4: Type of ordnance, if known (provide as much detail as possible about shape, color, condition, threat, and include initiation system [remote control, wire, or command detonated]). _____
_____
_____
_____

Line 5: CBRN contamination._____
_____
_____
_____

Line 6: Are resources threatened (facilities, equipment, or assets)? _____
_____
_____
_____

Line 7: Impact on mission. (Does it interfere with current operation?)_____

_____

_____

_____

Line 8: Protective measures. (What you have done to protect personnel and equipment?)_____

_____

_____

_____

Line 9: Recommended priority response for explosive ordnance disposal.____

_____

_____

_____

GLOSSARY

ACE report. Field report that identifies friendly or enemy Ammunition, Casualties, and Equipment.

adipocere. A crumbly white or unctuous brownish waxy substance that accumulates on the fatty parts of a human corpse (the cheeks, breasts, abdomen, and buttocks). It is produced when fats chemically react with water and hydrogen in the presence of bacterial enzymes, breaking down into fatty acids and soaps. Resistant to bacteria, it can protect a corpse, slowing decomposition.

AK-47. Cost-effective assault rifle developed in the former Soviet Union and used primarily by communist and developing countries.

AKM. Similar to the AK-47, the AKM is an assault rifle with a perforated folding stock of Chinese horseshoe design.

algor mortis. The equalizing of body temperature to the surrounding air after death.

anthrax. *Bacillus anthracis;* an odorless, very deadly, powder or liquid bacteria or zoological disease recognized as one of the top stealth killers of humankind; used in biological warfare or bioterrorism.

anti-tracking. Anti-Tracking are passive defensive techniques and tactics used by an element to maintain a low profile in order to elude and evade the opposition through deception.

azimuth. In navigation, a horizontal angle measured clockwise in a circle from a north-pointing baseline and measured in degrees or mils. In a circle of 6,400 mils or 360 degrees, the baseline is the line pointing due north at the 0/6400 mil and 0/360 degree mark.

BDU. Battle Dress Uniform; camouflaged field utility uniform of the US Armed Forces.

Bounding Overwatch. A type of squad-level military movement in which half of the team provides protective fire while the other half of the team moves forward to another overwatch position in actual or imminent contact with enemy forces.

Chase. The person or persons being sought or pursued.

claymore. Antipersonnel mine composed of C4 and pellets that emits a semicircular blast area to the front and rear; it can be self-detonated or set up as a booby trap.

coil search pattern. A method in which a Tracker conducts a detailed search of an area using a winding or unwinding pattern resembling a coil.

counter-tracking. Counter-Tracking are offensive violent techniques and tactics used by an element in order to prevent the Tracker from following, capturing, or eliminating the element.

coverman. In a military operation, the second person in a team or squad formation; provides protection for the point man; in a tracking team, the second Tracker.

DMZ. Demilitarized Zone; a thin geographic area or buffer zone that runs along the border separating two potentially hostile countries, declared by both countries to contain no military forces.

drone. A small, unmanned aircraft, normally equipped with cameras to provide real-time imagery.

earthworm cast. A trail of sand or dirt pellets deposited by worms as they travel over the ground.

EMT. Emergency Medical Technician; the medic in a military unit.

END-EX. END of EXercise; official end to a military exercise.

exfiltration. The act of crossing over into friendly territory.

fan search pattern. A method in which a Tracker conducts a detailed search by starting at a central point, moving outward, and looping back toward the central point in a pattern that resembles a fan.

fastrope. Intertwined rope, three inches in diameter and green in color, that allows a person to slide down from a helicopter without burning his hands, using his feet to brake. They come in 60-, 90-, and 120-foot lengths.

finger. Geographic formation consisting of a thin ridge that juts outward from a larger ridge and is surrounded on either side by steep draws.

F3-EAD. Find, Fix, Finish, Exploit, Analyze, and Disseminate. A US Army doctrine that states that every soldier is a sensor (E2S). The skill of Human Tracking embodies this fundamental US Army doctrine more than any present official Military Skill Identifier in any of the services combined.

GPS Global Positioning System; an instrument that utilizes positioning satellite signals to determine one's exact location anywhere in the world.

grid search pattern. A method in which a Tracker conducts a detailed search by crisscrossing an area in a grid-like pattern.

ground signs. Those signs appearing at ground level up to ankle level.

Happy Mound. A Korean burial site.

harbor site. Sleep or meal site, based on the naval term for the location at which a ship is harbored.

Huey. UH-1 utility helicopter used extensively in Vietnam for moving troops, wounded personnel, and supplies.

Immediate Action Drills. A predetermined set of actions that determine specific moves to take in reaction to hostile/enemy contact.

infiltration. The act of crossing over into enemy territory.

Initial Search Procedure. Search procedures used to reestablish the trail of a Chase by backtracking and making a wide circle around the last known sign.

inter-deduction. Interpretation-deduction; the interpretation of a sign based on deductive reasoning.

livor mortis. Discoloration of a body due to the settling of blood.

middle signs. Those signs appearing from ankle level to eye level.

Most Probable Search Area. Area through which the Chase is most likely to travel; arrived at by using deductive reasoning.

night vision goggles (NVG). A set of goggles fitted with an infrared sighting optical designed to enhance night visibility.

objective rallying point (ORP). The last rallying point prior to a final assault on an enemy position.

observer-controller. Graders and/or referees in military exercises; they maintain the integrity of players, ensure realism, and provide a detailed critique/after-action report at the end of the exercise.

OPFOR. OPposing FORces; friendly forces playing the part of enemy forces in a war game.

PACE. An informal field plan that provides team members their Primary, Alternate, Contingency, and Emergency actions, routes, or rendezvous locations.

PMI. Postmortem interval.

point man. In a military operation, the person in the front of a team or squad formation; provides frontal protection.

point of infiltration. The line at which a unit or patrol crosses over from friendly to enemy lines during a military operation.

pointer. Foliage that has been brushed, bent, or broken in the direction of travel.

postmortem interval (PMI). A predetermined sequence of stages that a decaying body experiences from the time of death to complete decomposition.

Probing Search Procedure. Search procedure used to reestablish the trail of a Chase by starting from a central location, probing outward, returning to the central location, and probing outward at a slightly different angle.

psychological warfare. Those actions taken in a hostile environment designed to demoralize the opposing forces.

putrefaction. The rotting of the body tissue after death.

rear security. In a military operation, the person who brings up the rear; provides protection to the team or squad from enemy approaching from the rear; covers signs left behind by the team.

rigor mortis. Stiffening of the body after death, occurring within one to twelve hours.

ROK. Republic of Korea; South Korea.

SALUTE. Brief field report which identifies enemy Size, Activity, Location, Uniform, Time, and Equipment.

sign. Any trace, object, or mark left directly or indirectly by a person and/ or his equipment that could indicate the direction of travel, location, or condition of the person leaving it.

SITREP. SITuational REPort.

SOG. Studies and Observation Group.

standard operating procedures (SOP). A written set of procedures that standardizes actions to be taken under a certain set of conditions.

stride. The distance between the left and right (fore and rear) footprint in a walking or running pattern.

Studies and Observation Group. A US Army unit that conducted covert special operations in Southeast Asia during the Vietnam War.

thermal imaging device. A device that enables a person to "see" heat sources at night or through fog, smoke, or other translucent objects.

TOP. Tracker Observation Procedures.

top signs. Those signs appearing at eye level and above.

T.R.A.C.K.E.R. Acronym describing the key points in the creed of the Tracker: Territorial, Resourceful, Aggressive, Conscious, Keen insight, Experience, Resilient.

Tracker Observation Procedures (TOP). A systematic method of searching for the Chase's trail. The most common methods include coil, Grid, and fan.

Tracking Patrol Report. Detailed report of a tracking expedition.

transfer. The relocation of dirt or mud from its original location.

Type 64 pistol. Short round pistol with silencer manufactured in and used primarily by communist or developing countries; similar to the US-made Browning 1900.

unconventional warfare. Small-scale, often covert operations conducted behind enemy lines, usually in the form of special operations or counter-guerrilla warfare against insurgents.

RECOMMENDED READING

Ardrey, Robert. *Territorial Imperative.* New York: Atheneum, 1966.

Australian Military Forces. *Patrolling And Tracking.* Boulder: Paladin Press, 1988.

Betser, Moshe, and Robert Rosenberg. *Secret Soldier: The True Life Story of Israel's Greatest Commando.* New York: Atlantic Monthly Press, 1966.

Bodziak, William J. *Footwear Impression Evidence.* CRC Press, 1999.

————. *Tire Tread and Tire Track Evidence.* CRC Press, 2008.

Brown, Tom, Jr. *Case Files of the Tracker.* New York: Berkley Publishing Group, 2003.

————. *Natural Observation and Tracking.* New York: Berkley Publishing Group, 1999.

————. *The Science and Art of Tracking.* New York: Berkley Publishing Group, 1999.

Burnham, Federick Russell. *Scouting in Two Continents.* Doubleday, Doran & Company, 1929.

Chapman, F. Spencer. *The Jungle Is Neutral.* Guilford, CT: Lyons Press, 2003.

Chesbro, Michael. *Wilderness Evasion.* Boulder: Paladin Press, 2002.

Crawford, A. George. *Manhunting: Reversing the Polarity of Warfare.* PublishAmerica, 2008.

Daly, Ron Reid. *Selous Scouts: Top Secret War.* Galago Publishing Pty, 1983.

Dickerson, H. R. P. *The Arab of the Desert.* London: George Allen & Unwin LTD, 1949.

Dix, Jay, and Michael Graham. *Time of Death, Decomposition and Identification: An Atlas.* Boca Raton: CRC Press, 2000.

Fuller, Gregg, Ed Johnson, and Robert J Koester. *Trackers and Dog Handlers in Search and Rescue.* DBS Production, 2000.

Grainger, D. H. *Don't Die in the Bundo.* Littlehamton Book Services, 1984.

Grayer, George Whitty, and Troy A. Lettieri. *Foot Print: An Aid to the Detection of Crime for the Police and Magistracy.* Templar Concepts Publications, 2011.

Gwynne, S. C. *Empire Of The Summer Moon.* New York: Scribner, 2010.

Hardin, Joel. *Tracker: Case Files & Adventures of a Professional Man Tracker.* 2004.

Harris, Marvin. *Cannibalism and Kings.* New York: Random House Inc., 1977.

Hayes, Stephen K. *The Mystic Arts of the Ninja: Ninja Aruki.* Chicago, IL: Contemporary Books, Inc., 1985.

———. *The Ninja and Their Secret Fighting Art.* Rutland, VT: Charles E. Tuttle Co., 1981.

Hooper, Jim. *Beneath the Visiting Moon.* Lexington Books, 1990.

Hurth, John. *The Combat Tracking Guide.* Stack Pole Books, 2012.

Lawrence, Eric. *The Operator's Tactical Pistol Shooting Manual.* Linesville, PA: Blackheart International, 2002.

Lawrence, Eric, and Mike Pannone. *Tactical Pistol Shooting: Your Guide to Tactics & Techniques That Work,* 2nd Edition. 2009.

Lettieri, Troy A. *Scout Tracker; Operational and Training Notes of a Special Forces Combat Tracker.* Templar Concepts Publications, 2011.

Liebenberg, Louis. *The Art of Tracking.* Cape Town, South Africa: Struik Publishers, 1990.

Osuna, Frederico S., and Jon R. Boyd. *Index Tracking.* Amethyst Moon Publishing, 2012.

Plaster, John L. *SOG: The Secret Wars of America's Commandos in Vietnam.* New York: Simon & Schuster, 1997.

Poole, John H. All Poole's books (concentration on small tactical elements).

Rottman, Gordon. *US Special Warfare Units in the Pacific Theater 1941–45: "Scouts, Raiders, Rangers and Reconnaissance Units."* Osprey Publishing, 2005.

Scott-Donelan, David. *Tactical Tracking Operations.* Boulder: Paladin Press, 1999.

Sexton, Mark. *The Tracker's Way: Ancient Art and Modern Applications.* Self-published, 2012.

Wells, Spencer. *The Journey of Man: A Genetic Odyssey.* Princeton: Princeton University Press, 2002.

Van Wyk, Peter. *Burnham: King of Scouts.* Trafford Publishing, 2003.

US Army. Reference Field Manuals:

FM 2-91.6   Soldier Surveillance and Reconnaissance – 2007

FM 3-05.222   Special Forces Sniper Training and Employment – 2003

FM 3-20.98   Reconnaissance Platoon – 2002

FM 3-21.8   The Infantry Rifle Platoon and Squad – 2007

FM 3-22.10   Sniper Training and Employment – 1994

FM 3-24.2   Tactics in Counter Insurgency – 2009

FM 3-34.119   Improvised Explosive Device Defeat – 2005

FM 3-55.93   Long Range Surveillance Unit Operations – 2008

FM 3-97.6   Mountain Operations

FM 7-92   The Infantry Reconnaissance Platoon and Squad – 1992

FM 7-42   Combat Tracker and Tracker Dog Training and Employment – 1973

FM 17-98   Scout Platoon – 1999

FM 19-20   Law Enforcement Investigation. Chapter 19, "Death."

FM 21-26   Map Reading and Land Navigation

FM 21-75   Combat Skills of the Marine – 1984

FM 90-3/FM 7-27   Desert Operations

FM 90-5   Jungle Operations

SH 21-76   Ranger Handbook

INDEX

ABOUT THE AUTHORS

David Diaz has taught human tracking and anti- and counter-tracking tactics, techniques, and procedures from the deserts, jungles, and mountains into the urban streets of six continents. He is a retired US Army Special Forces/Marine. Diaz has thirty years of experience in human tracking. His unique skill set has not only bolstered the efforts of US conventional and special operational units; he has also trained elements of various allied and NATO troops. Diaz is recognized throughout the military, law enforcement, other agencies, along with the petroleum, telecommunication, and mining industries, as a subject-matter expert in the theory and practice of human tracking.

Diaz provides a very realistic and challenging program of instruction that always exceeds the client's needs. He has fine-tuned his craft through many years of dedication and studying with the finest throughout the world, including the Dyaks/Iban of Brunei and Malaysia, Kiwi of New Zealand, Negritos aborigines of the Philippines, the San people of Botswana, and US Marine Vietnam veterans who learned their skill from the Montagnards of the highlands of Vietnam, Laos, and Cambodia. Diaz has also exchanged human tracking tactics, techniques, and procedures with the Sayerot Ha'Druim and Ha'Bedouin Trackers of Israel.

For four years he was exposed to the Rhodesian version of human tracking developed by Mr. Alan Savory. It's not beneath Diaz to have also learned from military privates and less reputable Trackers with innovative ideas. Due to his exposure to a broad and diverse range of teachings, he has developed various systematic approaches to the art and science of human tracking. Diaz has also written *Anti-Tracking: Hiding in the Shadows, The Illusion of Invisibility.* Presently, through a small 8(a) disabled veteran–owned business called Information Technology & Security Solutions Inc. ITS2, Diaz teaches exclusive small elements within the US military, NATO, Allied forces, and law enforcement.

Writer **V. L. McCann** has a BA in creative writing, having graduated with honors in 1981 and thereafter serving nearly twelve years as an officer in the US Army. In 1997, McCann became owner and chief writer/editor of Abbacy Professional Writing in Tacoma, Washington.